# RAISING THE DRAGON

## A Clarion Call to Welsh Rugby

*Robert Jones*

*With Huw Richards*

First published in Great Britain in 2001 by
Virgin Books
Thames Wharf Studios
Rainville Road
London W6 9HA

A catalogue record for the book is available from the British Library.

ISBN 1 85227 981 8

Typeset by TW Typesetting, Plymouth, Devon

Printed and bound in Great Britain by CPD Wales

# Contents

# Acknowledgements

Huw Richards would like to thank Paul McFarland for the initial introduction to Rob Jones. Rob Steen provided invaluable advice on the dark arts of ghost-writing and also the introduction to John Pawsey, whose contribution was above and beyond that normally demanded of a literary agent. Jonathan Taylor was a patient and supportive commissioning editor while Daniel Balado did a precise and perceptive job on the text. Ideas, advice and other support were provided by Gareth Williams, Peter Stead, Huw Bowen, Duncan Grant, Tim Glover, Thomas Davies, Paul Melly, Tom O'Sullivan and Kate Green. The staff of the Clinica Mutual de Seguridad, Calama, Chile ensured that writing this book remained physically possible. Thanks most of all to Rob, as fine a collaborator as a ghost-writer could wish for.

# 1 Trebanos Dreams

'Trebanos is no great size. It is a few miles north of Swansea, in the Swansea Valley. It isn't on every map, and you can walk to Clydach or Pontardawe, the two villages which join it at either end, in about five minutes. Visitors might say you can't really tell where Trebanos begins and ends, but that certainly doesn't apply to anyone who comes from the area. I always think of it as the typical Welsh village: it is in a valley, it used to have a coal mine and life centred around the pubs and the rugby clubs. There are a lot of places like that, and they are all special to the people who grew up in them. When I hear Cliff Morgan talk about Trebanog or Gareth Edwards about Gwaen-cae-Gurwen, I recognise in their sentiments the feelings I have for my village.'

In Paulie's Field where we used to play
The only crowd was a goat and horse,
The touchline prickly groves of gorse.
Piles of coats made our goals,
The hallowed turf was full of holes.
Yet we followed our heroes with every run
And played our games 'til the setting sun.

E VERYONE HAS A SPECIAL PLACE they remember from when they were young. For me and the kids of around my age in Trebanos in the 1970s, it was Paulie's Field. I couldn't even tell you why it was called that, but as my friend Geraint Thomas remembered in his poem 'The Champion of our Dreams', part of which is quoted above, it was our Cardiff Arms Park. From the time when I was first old enough to cross the road by myself, I must have spent about half my free time up there. The same goes for all the sportsmen who came out of Trebanos in that period: Bleddyn Bowen, who went on to captain his country and once played outside-half to me in an all-Trebanos half-back pairing for Wales, Greg Thomas, who played cricket for Glamorgan and England, and my brothers Anthony and Rhodri. They all played on Paulie's Field, they all have their memories of it.

It was up above the village, an old farm field, relatively flat. You had to walk up to it, past the council estate, which made it doubly convenient. If we weren't in Paulie's Field we'd be over at 'the counce'. It was where a lot of my friends were, and all of the action. It was quieter, with fewer cars around than at my end of the village and with more space to play. I'd go off after school and call on my friends in the estate, and we'd go up to the field.

We'd play rugby, cricket or whatever was the fashion of the moment; when some of us got interested in golf, we even devised a nine-hole course using the features of the field and finishing with a hole in the middle. We very rarely played football, which made very little impression on us, even when Swansea City were doing well in the Toshack years. If there was an England v. West Indies Test match on, we'd play that. One particularly strong, although not very enjoyable, memory is of being hit on the back of the head by a cork ball bowled by Greg Thomas, who is five years older than me (he was pretty quick even then). My friends had to carry me back home through Trebanos. The incident, however, gave me an early taste of notoriety: I'd see people pointing me out and hear them saying, 'There's the Jones boy who was hit on the head with a cricket ball.'

More often than not we played rugby, replaying the last international match or rehearsing the next one. A lot of the time we'd play Wales v. England. We all wanted to be Gareth Edwards, Barry John, Phil Bennett or (my particular hero) Gerald Davies, so there was never much demand to play for England. But whoever was there, and however many there were, we'd usually find a way of dividing ourselves into teams. Sometimes we'd play council houses v. private houses. On one occasion we organised a tournament and played for a cup we'd made ourselves, out of tinfoil.

This wasn't just something we did as small kids; we were up there most evenings when we were fourteen or fifteen. Paulie's Field is still there. I often walk up to it, but unfortunately children can't play there any more. The people who owned the land when I was a child were happy to allow us free access, but now the rules are different. Trebanos children have had to find somewhere else for their games.

One reason for going up there is for the view over the Swansea Valley and the village. It isn't the most spectacular panorama in the world, but I never get tired of it. It is the scene of many of my best and most important memories, not just of our games in Paulie's Field but of my life in Trebanos. I grew up in the village, and have always lived there. While you can never say never, I can't really imagine wanting to live anywhere else. The idea of packing up, moving out and going even five miles away just doesn't appeal to me.

I've never been happier on tour than when I've met somebody who comes from or knows Trebanos and there's a chance to talk about the village and sing its praises. My longest ever time away from Trebanos was in the mid-1990s when I was playing for Western Province in South Africa. I lived with my wife Meg and our daughter Emily in a wonderful apartment which had a classic picture-postcard view of Cape Town, one of the most beautiful, relaxing, laid-back cities I've ever visited. We'd look out at beautiful sunshine with a clear view of Table Mountain one way and whales playing a few hundred yards away in the sea on the other, and still – extraordinary as most people may find this – we'd miss Trebanos and feel homesick.

All my family live here. Rugby made me friends in many places around the world, and there are people like Anthony Clement, Paul Moriarty and Stuart Davies, all team-mates for years at Swansea, whose friendships are as close and important to me as anyone's. But a lot of my friends still come from and live in the village. It is where I am happiest and most comfortable, surrounded by people I know I can rely on and places that are familiar. Stuart Barnes once wrote that I had 'an insane degree of national fervour'. One reason why my feelings for Wales are so strong is that they are an extension of my feelings for Trebanos.

Trebanos is no great size. It is a few miles north of Swansea, in the Swansea Valley. It isn't on every map, and you can walk to Clydach or Pontardawe, the two villages which join it at either end, in about five minutes. Visitors might say you can't really tell where Trebanos begins and ends, but that certainly doesn't apply to anyone who comes from the area. I always think of it as the typical Welsh village: it is in a valley, it used to have a coal mine and life centred around the pubs and the rugby clubs. There are a lot of places like that, and they are all special to the people who grew up in them. When I hear Cliff Morgan talk about Trebanog or Gareth Edwards about Gwaen-cae-Gurwen, I recognise in their sentiments the feelings I have for my village.

My father, Cliff, worked as an electrician in the pit in the village, the Darren pit, until it closed in the mid-1960s. But at that time there was not much unemployment around; some, like my father, went to work for British Steel, and there were thousands of people working at the Mond Nickel works just down the road in Clydach, although I don't think there are more than a few hundred there now.

In the Max Boyce song about pits closing, the pithead baths became a supermarket; in Trebanos, they became the club-house for the rugby club. In those days there were two pubs in the village – the Pheasant and the Colliers – and the working men's club. The Colliers is still there and the working men's club is hanging on, but the Pheasant has been through a few changes. It was a football club for a while, but that has now closed and the rugby club is planning to move there after 32 years in the old pithead baths.

Life for us revolved around the rugby club, which played – and still does – in Trebanos Park, down at the bottom of the village by the river. We occasionally went to see Swansea at St Helen's or Llanelli at Stradey – I was taken to my first games at seven or eight – but most of the first-class rugby we watched was on television. Most Saturday afternoons were spent down at the park, watching Trebanos play in the West Wales Rugby Union Championship. The crowds weren't that massive – perhaps there would be a hundred or so – but you could be sure of finding half a dozen or so of us youngsters playing our own match down by the side of the pitch or behind the posts.

This area of Wales was, and is, a real rugby hotbed. Glais, Vardre and Pontardawe, all strong West Wales clubs, were only a mile or so away and, in the same valley, all within a few miles of each other, you can find Morriston, Alltwen, Cwmgors, Brynammen Cwmllynfell, Cwmtwrch, Abercrave and Ystradgynlais, each club with its own strong sense of identity, its history and love of the game. Trebanos had a reasonably strong team to compete with these sides; there were normally Trebanos players in the West Wales District XV, the local representative fifteen. I looked up to them as much as I did to international players because they were that much more real to me. I saw them play regularly and knew them off the field as well. There was a whole family of Penhales – Clive, Lyn and Viv – all of whom were excellent players; Keith Williams, who was a really tough, aggressive back-row forward; and a very small, quick winger who was always known as 'Spike' – it was years before I found out his real name. As a youngster I just could not understand why he was not playing for one of the big clubs.

Later on, of course, there were Trebanos players who went on to the top. By the time I left school I was already playing for Swansea, so I never played for the senior Trebanos team, but Bleddyn Bowen played for a while and set the record for most points scored in a single match, a record later broken by Arwel Thomas during the half season or so he played before being spotted by Neath. There can't be many village clubs where a points-scoring record has passed from one future Welsh international to another.

There always were players who had real talent, but who were also happy to enjoy their rugby at that level, content to regard their game on a Saturday as an enjoyable break from the week's work rather than go through all the pressures and commitments involved in playing first-class rugby. My father was like that. He played outside-half for Trebanos and had a few games for Neath, and his brother, my uncle Gerald, was scrum-half for the village. People have told me that both of them were really talented players, but Dad's commitment was to his three children – my older brother Anthony, me and my younger brother Rhodri – to give us the chance to play rugby as well as we possibly could.

So coming from and living in such a close family, I don't have to look very far to know why I feel so strongly about Trebanos. My father has three brothers and one sister. One died young, but the others still live in the village. Of their ten children only one has moved away, and now there are around a dozen grandchildren. It was never a matter of travelling to a cousin's birthday party when I was a child – all we had to do was walk up the road. Today I still have nine cousins living within five minutes' walk of my house. My mother, Marion (née Griffiths), came from just down the road in Clydach. One of her brothers, my Uncle Cyril, followed his father (my grandfather) into the Mond nickel works where he spent all his working life. Her other brother, my Uncle Russell, boxed for Wales as a heavyweight. I didn't inherit any of the size from that side of the family (although my mother isn't that big), but there are a few Australians who'd say my performances for the Lions in 1989 showed that I had learned something from my uncle!

Apart from one year down close to the the rugby club-house, I have lived all my life in Swansea Road. When Meg and I were married the papers made a lot of the fact that I was moving just twelve doors away from my parents. Now we are closer than that. The little road where I now live sits on land my father and his brother bought in the late 1960s. The first three houses they built on it were for family – the first for their sister and two for themselves; now there are seven there. Ours, at the end, was the last to be built, next to my cousins. My aunt, at the other end, has moved out, but only to be nearer her children, who live elsewhere in Trebanos. As a family, we don't seem to get itchy feet. Meg comes from a similarly close-knit family and community in Upper Cwmtwrch.

As I said, my father wanted the best for his children, to give us opportunities he perhaps had never had. There was never any pressure on us to play rugby, we were never told that we had to do things, but he was always there to encourage us, ready to go out to practise passing or kicking and to offer advice on the best way of doing it. When we got keen on cricket, he put up a net in the back garden with fencing around it and laid an old colliery conveyor belt along the floor. It wasn't a full-size wicket, but it was big enough for him to stand at the far end and bowl to us. Perhaps as a result, we all played cricket well at school; in fact, Anthony played at county level and Rhodri played for Wales Schools in the under-11 age group. In the winter, it doubled up as a passing net for rugby practice.

One Christmas, when I was about eight or nine, I was given a new size three rugby ball. It was wet and windy outside – not completely unusual for the Swansea Valley in December – so we couldn't go out to play. My father moved back all the furniture in the living room so that we could practise passing indoors. We played a lot of rugby in that living room – and we didn't need a proper ball to practise. A couple of rugby socks would roll up very nicely, and I'd practise goalkicking over the curtains or we'd play matches behind the settee. Of course, by that time I had already watched my first Wales match, on the television in my uncle's house next door when I was about six or seven. Barry John was playing, and it was Wales against Scotland, but I don't remember the score. What I do remember is that, although I wasn't sitting still all the time – I'd jump up with everyone else whenever Wales scored – I had never before sat for so long in the same place or stayed focused for so long on the same thing.

We couldn't have had more support from our parents. Over the years, my mother was presented with endless amounts of dirty kit to wash, and she was always determined that her children should play in the whitest shorts in the whole school. Whenever any of us – first Anthony, then me, and now Rhodri – was playing, they'd be there to support us. Dad was particularly good at arranging his job around our matches when he was a manager at British Steel. If I was playing in a sevens tournament at Solihull, for instance, he would arrange a work meeting in Birmingham. Geoff Davies, the teacher at Cwmtawe School who has been so important to my life in rugby, used to say, 'I'd love to have your father's job.' For years they had no holidays, instead spending their time and money travelling to follow our rugby matches.

Dad also started a junior side at Trebanos to give me and my friends more rugby. We played under-13 games at school on Wednesdays, but there were no Saturday games. Trebanos hadn't had a junior section before, but Dad got together with a few people, started a team and got it accepted into the Swansea and District Union. It served a real purpose. We had a good side, winning several sevens tournaments and getting to the final of the District under-13 competition. Our under-15s got to their final in the first year. We enjoyed those games enormously and were in a position to challenge anyone in the area.

As I was enjoying junior rugby, Anthony, three and a half years older than me, was starting to get noticed as a player. He was also a scrum-half, different in style to me because he was stocky, strong and quite physical. He was also very committed to his rugby. I always enjoyed going out and playing, but as a schoolkid I wasn't quite so keen on slogging my guts out in training. Ant was much more dedicated in that way. He even bought himself an old set of weights. My mother talks about how she would come home, find me eating chocolate in front of the television and Ant out in the kitchen, where he'd set up the weights because it was wet outside.

Looking back, I realise how important an inspiration Ant was. I'd see him come home with a cap or a trophy, and I'd think, 'I want to do that as well.' I remember him scoring a try in the corner at Murrayfield for Wales against Scotland at under-18 level. I felt real pride in his achievement; I thought that there really couldn't be anything better than playing and scoring for Wales. I still have those same feelings today when I see how hard Rhodri works at his game, or when he plays well for Swansea.

We spoke English at home, although both my parents speak Welsh. There was always a lot of Welsh spoken in Trebanos, so I have always spoken the language, although there have been, and still are, times when I would like to be more fluent – like at school, where some of the teachers spoke English, some Welsh and so you had lessons in both languages. The rugby staff, Eifion Price and Owen Roberts, were both Welsh-speakers, so a lot of my early conversations about the game of rugby were conducted in Welsh. Their advice and encouragement were very important to me right at the start. That doesn't mean I didn't get into trouble though, and they were both pretty strict whenever I stepped out of line. I must have been smacked with the slipper – an old gym shoe with a handle on it – at least half a dozen times, and there were other times when I was smacked or caned. But it was at that school that I had my first hint that I might be good at rugby.

When you start playing, you don't really know – you just enjoy the game. Then, at the age of eight, when I was in what they called Standard Two, I was chosen to play for the under-11 team. I remember playing down at Trebanos Park against the Wern School from Ystalyfera. I was put at outside-half, and I suppose from then on I realised deep down that I might be better than average. The year after, as a nine-year-old, I was chosen to play for Swansea Valley under-11s. Then, at the age of ten, came an invitation to play for West Glamorgan. That was the pattern of my early years of rugby – I often seemed to be a year or two ahead, although I had to wait until I was 11 to play for West Wales under-11s.

The school is a hugely important part of our community, part of my memories and Meg's (she worked there as a nursery nurse). We lost it for a while when the school was moved to Clydach as a result of subsidence from the old pit workings, which made the existing buildings unsafe. Having a school in the village matters enormously in terms of securing the future of the community, so I was very happy to be involved in the campaign to bring the school back, which succeeded in 1997. Some people, particularly Hywel Griffiths, did a huge amount of work in support of that campaign and deserve the credit for its success. I am still a governor of the school and a great deal of teaching there is conducted in Welsh, but my daughter, Emily, now goes to another school, Ysgol Gynredd in Pontardawe, which has an even stronger focus on Welsh. It was a difficult decision to make, but people in the village understood that we made the switch for Emily's benefit. The preservation of Welsh culture and language is very important to me, and we want our children to have the best possible understanding of them.

At that school, I met the group of friends with whom I would go up to Paulie's Field. We met in the early 1970s when we were around six years old and stuck together all the way through school – wherever I was you'd probably find Geraint Thomas, Mark Strong Edwards, Byron Temblett, Andrew Morgan (who for some reason was always known as 'Pogso'), Carl Evans, Keith Morgan (who lived just over the road from me), Chris Francis and Nigel Doyle. Most of them still live in the village. If I go down to the park to watch Trebanos play on a Saturday or into the club bar for a drink in the evening, there's a good chance some of them will be there. Some are married to girls they met at school or in the village, and our families and children have become friends as well, strengthening the bond.

There's also a good chance I'll meet my cousins on a Saturday or Sunday, kicking a ball around in Trebanos Park with their sons – the next generation of Jones rugby players from Trebanos – as my father used to kick a ball around with me, Ant and Rhod. My cousin Justin's son Nathan played for West Wales under-11s last year at scrum-half and is now at Cwmtawe, the secondary school we all went to. His brother Ross looks like being a useful player as well, although he's still trying to find his position. Justin's brother Craig has a son called Rhys. He's a scrum-half as well, but goes to a neighbouring school called Alltwen. And just to make absolutely sure that the supply of Jones scrum-halves from Trebanos does not give out, my father is already working to make sure that my son, Tiaan, who is still a toddler, will be able to kick equally well with both feet.

I know how much Trebanos people care about their rugby, how much pride they took in the successes of the 1970s and how much disappointment they have felt during the lean years since. There was real pride in the achievements of Trebanos boys who played for Wales – all of us have known, however badly things were going wrong for the team and however much criticism we were getting, that we could count on the support of our own community. That pride was never more on display than when Bleddyn Bowen and I came back from the World Cup in 1987. Both of us were expecting to go straight home, but we were met by our fiancées – neither of us was married then – in Ynystawe and taken back to the rugby club for a celebration party. There were huge crowds waiting for us at the crossroads by the Colliers Arms, and the clubhouse was packed. Most of the village seemed to be there: our families, people with whom we'd grown up and been at school, players we had watched when we were children, the older people to whom we used to listen when they talked about rugby in the clubhouse – just about everybody.

Geraint Thomas wrote his poem 'The Champion of our Dreams' about watching me play for Wales and remembering when we used to play together up in Paulie's Field. In my testimonial brochure he explained that he had used the word 'champion' to mean 'one who carries a cause on behalf of others', and went on to say, 'It is every child's dream to play for his country, and when Rob ran out for Wales, each one of us was out there with him.' Playing for Wales was indeed always my greatest aspiration – if I am honest, my only aspiration – and when I achieved it I was conscious of the overwhelming support of my friends, family and community. When I was playing for Wales, I was also playing for Trebanos.

Playing for Wales is one dream, an individual one I was lucky enough to be able to fulfil; another dream, which we all share, is for Wales once again to be a leading rugby nation, playing the game with the imagination, skill and intelligence we once regarded as our own special qualities. That would bring me and other people in Trebanos as much pleasure as the fulfilment of my own personal dream did. And I believe strongly that it can be done. This book will allow me to explain how I think it can be done, at the same time as showing how, during my period as a player for Swansea, Bristol, Cardiff, Wales and the Lions, we fell from the standards we used to set ourselves, so far that the dream at times started to look and feel rather more like a nightmare. But, as I said, I have no doubt that Wales can be great again. The people of Trebanos, and the many other communities the length and breadth of our country who cherish their rugby at both local and national level, deserve no less.

# **2** Raising the Dragon

'The display of individual skill was at its height in the 1970s, when Wales had players like Gareth Edwards, Phil Bennett, Barry John and Gerald Davies who had real magic in their play, the ability to do things others could not. And there were others who had the full range of skills. They gave us a team which was regarded as one of the world's best, if not the best. Wales is not the most confident nation in the world, but their play made us feel we were at least as good as the people at the other end of the Severn Bridge and on the other side of the Channel.'

P ERHAPS RUGBY SHOULD NOT MATTER to us as much as it does. It is a sport, after all, not a matter of life and death. Something like the steel closures in early 2001, putting thousands of people in Wales out of work, should certainly put things into perspective. But rugby has been an important part of Welsh life for almost as long as the game has been played here, certainly since our national team had its first successes. You could say it is ingrained into Welsh life, that it is important not just as a sport in which we can show we are as good as or better than bigger and richer countries, but for the effect it has on the nation's mood.

Individuals, groups and whole communities suffer when Wales play poorly. On the other hand, if there is any success – either when individuals from a community win a place in the national team, or when the team itself wins – the mood changes quickly and dramatically. If we are successful on the field, whether as clubs doing well domestically or in Europe, or as the national team winning in the Six Nations or World Cup, the spirits of the entire nation are lifted. Whether or not we think a sport should be taken so seriously is largely imma- terial. Rugby is an incredibly important part of Welsh life.

That pride in ourselves as a rugby nation has been built up over a long period, by great teams and remarkable players. We haven't always had the biggest or strongest players or been the best at sitting down and analysing how the game should be played. What we have been good at is developing talented players, good footballers with vision who can deceive opponents, create opportunities and use their skills to put team-mates into space. Those individual skills have always been a very important part of the appeal and success of the game in Wales.

The display of individual skill was at its height in the 1970s, when Wales had players like Gareth Edwards, Phil Bennett, Barry John and Gerald Davies who had real magic in their play, the ability to do things others could not. And there were others who had the full range of skills. They gave us a team which was regarded as one of the world's best, if not the best. Wales is not the most confident nation in the world, but their play made us feel we were at least as good as the people at the other end of the Severn Bridge and on the other side of the Channel.

You can look back to earlier times and see Welsh players who had that vision and imagination. If you watch film of Bleddyn Williams side-stepping or Clem Thomas cross-kicking to set up the winning try against the All Blacks in 1953, the last time we beat them, you see players with terrific instinctive skills. There has always been that outside-half factor in Welsh rugby, people like Cliff Morgan, Barry John and Jonathan Davies. There was a reason why Barry was known as 'King John' and Jonathan was known through-out the rugby world as 'The Wizard': these were expressions that tried to capture some of the sheer magic in their play, their ability to do totally unpredictable things nobody else would even so much as try, and reflected the admiration with which they and the best of the Welsh game were regarded throughout the world. If you look at our best teams, they always featured two or three players like that. The others would not be quite at that level – it is impossible to imagine a team with fifteen players like that – but they would be skilful, capable of thinking on their feet and taking decisions for themselves, and would have been given the freedom to do this.

Now I am not suggesting that these qualities are peculiar to Wales and Welsh players. Every serious rugby nation produces great, creative, imaginative players. Throughout my career we suffered at the hands of All Black teams who had these qualities in abundance. The French have always had them. Scotland have had a tradition of producing gifted all-round footballers – not just backs like Gregor Townsend but forwards like David Sole, Colin Deans, Finlay Calder, John Jeffrey and Derek White, all of whom did their specialised jobs exceptionally well and had the footballing skills to match. Scotland have always been very good at bringing out the best in the talent they have. Ireland, too, are now showing these qualities through players like Peter Stringer, Ronan O'Gara and Brian O'Driscoll, and you won't find a forward with better all-round skills than Keith Wood. At the beginning of my career we were always confident that we'd have the edge on England in terms of footballing skill, but with Clive Woodward giving players like Mike Catt and Jonny Wilkinson the freedom any player needs to do well, we certainly can't say that any more.

I am not saying that you can win rugby matches with flair alone. Perhaps that was the case once, and we relied on our talent to stay ahead of our opponents in Britain, but we now live in a much more complex and sophisticated sporting world. Coaches have a much wider range of forms of analysis open to them, such as the videos which my former Wales Schools captain Alun Carter prepares to assist Graham Henry and the Welsh squad, and, as full-time professionals, the coaches and players have the time to use them. Nutritionists, sports scientists and other experts are on hand to advise players. All of these have their uses, provided we do not forget the prime importance of the imagination and skills of the individual player.

Good teams also need organisation and discipline, particularly in defence and in the set-pieces: scrum and line-out. Good teams have always had a decent forward platform. You don't need to tell a former scrum-half how difficult it is for a team to play when the forwards are not winning good possession. So I am certainly not advocating that Welsh teams should throw caution to the wind and try to run the ball from everywhere, whatever the conditions, opposition and circumstances. Indeed, my argument is the opposite of that: teams should not do anything irrespective of conditions, opposition and circumstances. What the players should have is the ability to adjust the way they play, and the skills to make that adjustment effective in terms of winning the match.

A good example of that was our win over England at Cardiff in March 1989. We didn't go out with the plan that I should spend the game box-kicking, but early in the game we realised that Jon Webb and Rory Underwood, the England full-back and wing, were vulnerable to the tactic. At the same time, Bob Norster was in complete control in the line-out, so we were winning a lot of possession in that area of the field. We adjusted the way we played and as a result won a game most people had expected us to lose.

My concern is that we are losing those qualities that once made us good. But Welsh rugby has a number of problems that need addressing. We need to get our structures right, both in terms of player development and relations between clubs and the union. We need to start producing players with the desire to be the best, with the sort of hunger I saw in young South African players during my time at Western Province. As a nation, I think we accept second best too easily, and we have to change that. All of this is likely to take a while; it is probably a ten-year job rather than something which will affect the country's performance at the 2003 World Cup in Australia.

Most of all, though, we need to allow our players to play with freedom, to use their instinctive skills and to develop. Rugby is not chess or American football. You can't programme players. If you try to do it they become predictable, lose their instincts and the ability to think on their feet. And if we lose that, we lose much of what makes rugby a worthwhile game. The best moments for a spectator are those which spring from instinctive skill: the pass which puts the man outside into space, the side-step which takes a runner away from his marker, the sudden change of direction which catches the opposition unawares. They aren't the only points of interest, of course – as a fan or player you can admire good scrummaging, rucking or tackling, a well-executed line-out routine or a well-planned set move – but they do more than anything else to make the game attractive. They are also the best moments for players. As a player, I wanted to be involved as much as possible, to be making my own decisions, following my instincts and trying to outwit the opposition. Take that away, reduce the player's role to one of simply doing what the coach has told him, and you make it a much less interesting game to play.

I am concerned that players are being stifled in this way, in particular that this philosophy is now creeping down from the senior game into the junior ranks. I'll give you a very worrying example. One young player I spoke to had been criticised after a not very effective performance in a representative match. He had been told before the match that at scrums the number eight would pick up and try to cross the gainline. If that didn't work, the scrum-half's job on the second phase was to offload to another forward or his outside-half. There was no thought of him using his instincts, of him looking around and taking the best option according to his judgement of the situation. Part of this player's frustration was that running was the strongest part of his game, and he was effectively being encouraged not to use it.

There are teams that are programmed as to what to do on the first, second and third phase. If those plans don't work, there is something laid down for the fourth phase, and then on the fifth there's something else. I know you have to have some structure and organisation, but this sort of approach is going way too far. The young player I was talking to is being deprived of the chance to use his initiative, not to mention the best aspect of his game. Players who simply do what they are told all the time will lose any sense of invention. Rather than developing his talent, this player's coach is far more likely to destroy it – along with his enthusiasm for the game.

Players must be encouraged to develop all-round skills, not just those which are specific to their position. This is as important for forwards as it is for backs. When I see film of matches from the 1970s I am reminded that good rugby isn't just about great backs. Forwards like John Taylor and Mervyn Davies had all-round footballing skills as well. One of my concerns is that we have stopped encouraging players to make the best of all their skills, instead expecting them just to concentrate on the main features of their game.

I remember David Young when he first came into the Swansea team as a young player. He was a terrific, dynamic player, a real all-round footballer who had everything. He could handle well, and he contributed to so many aspects of our play – I remember seeing him once charge down a kick by diving at the ball. Of course scrummaging was always his primary job, and he did it very well (he still does), but the other parts of his game seem to have fallen by the wayside over the years, I would guess because he hasn't been encouraged to develop them. You don't simply lose that sort of footballing ability overnight. Dai has been an exceptional player anyway, but had he been encouraged to cultivate his skills and his rugby know-how he would have been an even better player.

Scott Quinnell is another Welsh forward with much greater footballing ability than has been obvious during a lot of his time in a red jersey. As he showed by setting up Robert Howley's try in Paris during the 2001 Six Nations, he has a good pair of hands and a good footballing brain. He knows when to pass, when not to pass, and how to put the man outside him into space, but for too much of the time we have used him as a sort of human battering ram, too often trying to exploit his ability to cross the gainline, and it has made Welsh play too predictable.

The example of the benefit you get from encouraging football skills in forwards is provided by Darren Morris. You couldn't possibly complain about the way he goes about his main job because he is an excellent scrummager. But his worth to Swansea and Wales goes well beyond that. He is quick for a big man and has real footballing ability, more than capable of making a break and offloading so that the man outside him is put into space. He has taken a little while to show those qualities for Wales, but now they are beginning to come through.

My own position of scrum-half also illustrates this need to focus more on developing skills. Something that is not always recognised as a vital element in a scrum-half's game, but which I believe in totally, is the ability to kick equally well with both feet in defence or attack. You may only have to use your weaker foot once a match or every couple of matches, but if you can't use it at all you can be certain that at some stage you will be caught out, landing your team in trouble. If you can't kick well off either foot, you are much less likely to be able to take the pressure off your outside-half. The skill gives you extra attacking options and, perhaps most importantly of all, confidence that you will be able to cope with almost any situation. Sometimes when we think an outside-half is having a poor game it is because his scrum-half can't kick well enough to take responsibility on his own shoulders, and the outside-half is getting ball which puts him under pressure.

I always feel sympathy for scrum-halves who are naturally left-footed – Paul John, Ryan Powell and Richard Smith are Welsh examples, and Joost van der Westhuizen is also left-footed. In attacking positions a scrum-half needs to be able to kick well with his right foot, so they are at a disadvantage. The benefit, however, is that the left-footed player works hard to learn how to play with his right foot too, whereas right-footed players can get away with more and may not work sufficiently hard at developing their weaker foot. Rob Howley, for instance, should really be able to kick better than he does off his left foot. I've seen him put himself in some really awkward positions trying to avoid using it. And this weakness is more common than you might expect among the world's top scrum-halves; you rarely see Australia's

George Gregan kick with his left, and the All Black Justin Marshall doesn't do it terribly well either. The result is that too much reliance is placed on the outside-half's boot, kicking either tactically or to relieve pressure.

Ultimately, though, the key element in any scrum-half's game is the ability to move the ball quickly. That always has to come first. There's been a periodic tendency in Wales, not least during my career, to opt for physical power over other scrum-half attributes. Perhaps that is natural during times when confidence is low, to reach for physical strength as a sort of safety blanket. When your forwards aren't delivering sufficiently good ball, there is a sort of logic in going for a scrum-half who plays like another loose forward and may be able to turn bad ball into good through physical aggression, and I certainly would not argue that there is no place for this style of player. Terry Holmes, for instance, did a terrific job for Wales and was the dominant figure in the team before he went to rugby league. The combative Gary Armstrong has been a major figure for Scotland over the last decade and more.

But ultimately, I believe we have to show confidence in our own wit and native ability, and keep faith with the classic style of scrum-half. It has been argued that the game nowadays is harder and more muscular. I've got no argument with that – anyone who wants to play international rugby has to be able to reach the levels of physical fitness required. You have to be able to tackle, but that is a matter of technique as much as strength. I always enjoyed tackling and rather relished bringing down players who were much bigger than me, which was just as well as most of them were. Defences are fitter and better organised than they used to be, so there are fewer openings. But that has not reduced the need for players who move the ball quickly and have the vision to take the right options. Quite the opposite. If there is limited space and few opportunities it is that much more important that you have players capable of making the most of them. Top-class rugby is now more than ever a game in which inches and split seconds make a difference – the pass which gets there slightly more quickly or at a more sympathetic angle to the player who is trying to make a break is often the difference between getting through and being tackled.

The last thing you need in the modern environment is the tactical straitjacket put on the young scrum-half I referred to earlier. A scrum-half has to be encouraged to develop an instinctive understanding with his two key team-mates, the outside-half and the number eight. It used to be said that I could find Jonathan Davies in a darkened room (he would certainly not have been slow about letting me know where he was and how he wanted the ball!), and we see that sort of relationship between the Irish half-backs Peter Stringer and Ronan O'Gara, who have been playing together since they were seven. Stringer has the skill to put a pass in the ideal position in front of his man so that he can hit the gap at pace, and – an even more important quality – the vision to see where that gap is in the first place.

In terms of the scrum-half/number eight dynamic, I was hugely impressed as a young player by the way in which Dave Loveridge and Murray Mexted worked together for the All Blacks. I remember when I was about sixteen watching the *Focus on Rugby* television programme, a coaching series which spotlighted a different position each week, and being fascinated by their play. Loveridge was a natural model for me – there was no point in my trying to play like Gareth Edwards or Terry Holmes with my build – and I don't think I've ever seen a scrum-half who could create so much space for his team-mates. He and Mexted knew each other's games inside out and worked brilliantly together. Zinzan Brooke and Graham Bachop did it pretty well for New Zealand too.

You can't programme that sort of relationship or instruct players on how to react given certain situations. Taking the right option in play comes from developing an understanding of the strengths and weaknesses of each other's game. Number eight Stuart Davies and I built up a good understanding of each other's game by playing together for years at

Swansea. Stuart wasn't the quickest player in the world, but he was very strong. He had the knack of taking on the opposition back row, tying in a couple of defenders and still managing to offload the ball, creating the space for a break. We talked a great deal – part of the scrum-half's job is to be the eyes and ears of the pack when they are head-down in a scrum or maul. Some of the time I would tell Stuart there was an opportunity for him to pick up and go, at other times he would be talking to me. We might release the ball slowly to keep the opposition back row down, or quickly to get them charging at our outside-half, which would create some space for me. The point about this is that none of it was pre-programmed. We did not always take the right option or execute it well, but the important thing was that we were allowed to try. Mike Ruddock, our coach, did not tell us what to do. It was simply a matter of using our judgement, based on skill, knowledge and an instinctive understanding built up over several years of playing together.

Indeed, the coach has a vitally important role to play here. He is a guide, an adviser and an analyst. A good coach can make a huge difference to a team; so, unfortunately, can a bad one. The best ones have a real knowledge of the game, sharp analytical skills and good man-management. They also have the confidence to allow players to make their own judgements, to take their own decisions on the pitch. As Gerald Davies once said, 'A coach can tell you how to do something, but not when to do it.' Bad coaches try to tell you how and under what circumstances to do everything, which in the heat of battle often leaves players thinking 'Right, what am I supposed to do here?' when they should be making an instinctive play. The best coaches, people like Ian McGeechan, Mike Ruddock and Tony Gray, always give their players the freedom to think and play.

There is always an element of risk in this, of course, but as Daryl Jones once said while he was coaching at Bristol, 'If you come off the field without making any mistakes, I'll be on your back, because the only way not to make mistakes is not to try anything.' I don't think it is a fluke that Daryl has consistently been associated with the development of bright, talented young players both at Neath College and at the Neath club where he won a Welsh championship in 1996 with a team full of young players playing good rugby. He was prepared to place confidence in them when a less imaginative coach would have been telling them in detail what to do, or opting instead to field more experienced players.

Wales also need to show faith in players who are capable of doing the unusual. Players like Mark Ring and Arwel Thomas can occasionally be difficult to play with because it is so hard to guess what they are going to do next, but opponents as well as team-mates can be caught out. The teams Mark and Arwel have played for have generally come out well ahead of the game on their performances. One of the challenges for coaches all over the world is to find a way to incorporate gifted but unpredictable players into a team pattern, while players with instinctive skills of their own should be able to adjust to them.

To understand the benefits players like that can bring, we need only think of the try Wales scored in the first few minutes at Twickenham in February 1996. There were three simple points on offer, but Arwel saw that England had relaxed, waiting for the kick to be taken, and he took a quick tap penalty from which we scored. By exercising his instinctive judgement, he won his country seven points instead of three and inspired a performance that brought Wales closer to winning at Twickenham than we had been for some eight years.

We can also go back to one of the best remembered incidents in my career, against Scotland at Cardiff in that Triple Crown year of 1988 when Jonathan Davies caught a pass which was going above his head, kicked ahead and scored. The truth is that I didn't throw a bad pass at all – I deliberately lobbed the ball up to draw the Scottish defenders on to him, knowing he would realise that a kick ahead would put him into a position from which he could score. At least that's my story, and I'm sticking to it! Jonathan, of course, will tell you a different story. He'd say, 'Well, at least you got it there.'

The serious point here is that Jonathan, put into a difficult situation as he received the ball, reacted instinctively and a remarkable try was scored. We need to see more of that sort of thing, but coaches have to learn to trust their players first, to trust in their instincts. For Wales, this means identifying our best players, placing that trust in them and then playing to their strengths. In Neil Jenkins we have one of the best passers of a ball in world rugby, while Mark Taylor is probably better at making an outside break than anyone in Britain at the moment. Why, then, aren't we seeing that long, flat pass of Neil's used to put Mark in positions where he can make breaks?

I don't share the concerns some people have about playing people out of their regular position, so long as they have the skills and attributes necessary to play effectively there. Tony Clement had hardly ever played at full-back before he was selected to play there against England in February 1988, but his attacking skills added a fresh dimension to the team. Mike Catt has played for England just about everywhere in the back division except for scrum-half, and has generally been an outside-half for Bath. That hasn't stopped him being highly effective as an inside-centre for England, where the vision and skills he has developed as an outside-half give his side an extra playmaker and a whole new range of options.

I am well aware of the handicaps we face in Wales. We have many fewer players to choose from than other countries like New Zealand, South Africa, England and France. Even at our best, in the 1970s, we could not beat New Zealand by ourselves, and it wasn't until two years ago, at the twelfth attempt in nearly a hundred years, that we beat South Africa. It will always be tough to beat the top southern hemisphere countries, and England have been consistently strong for the last decade and have adjusted far better to professionalism than we have. Yet I can't help noticing that we got a lot closer to the likes of South Africa and New Zealand in the days when we trusted to our instincts and skills. Australia don't have anything like the number of players we have, let alone as many as the four largest countries, yet they have won two World Cups and been consistently strong since the mid-1980s. And it wasn't many years before then that they asked Ray Williams, our national coaching organiser, to go out there to explain the Welsh coaching system, which just goes to show that countries can turn around their fortunes.

It won't be easy. It won't happen overnight. But it can happen. I do not accept the argument that we haven't got the players to compete with the rest of the world. Given the right structures, encouragement and attitudes, I believe Welsh players can be as good as any in the world, just as they have been at times in the past. Of course that cannot be accomplished simply by changing things around the Wales team itself. The national XV is the end result, the culmination of the processes of the structure and the system. If that structure does not work, if that system is failing, then so will the national team.

We must look at the way we organise rugby in Wales, in particular at how we develop players. This will have implications at club level, where there are serious issues around the structure of the season. Clubs must also adjust to professionalism, in particular to their responsibilities as employers of young men, many of them just out of school. We have to be able to offer our players not only a decent living from the game, but the chance to develop the skills which will take them through their lives after they finish playing. And we need to go back further than that, to the youngest players who are just being introduced to the game. It is essential they are given the right start.

# **3** Starting Out

'It is good that there are lots of youngsters playing the game – all children should be encouraged to play team sports because team activities encourage the development of social skills, communication and the ability to work with other people – but too much pressure is being placed on them too young. It worries me when I hear of eight- and nine-year-olds playing in competitions; it depresses me when I visit clubs' junior sections to hear talk of building winning teams and maintaining unbeaten records. At that age the emphasis should be entirely on enjoying the game and building a few skills. These kids are too young to be getting competitive – the emphasis is all wrong.'

I HAVE ALWAYS ENJOYED MY RUGBY. This doesn't, of course, mean that there weren't occasions when I was disappointed because I or the team had played badly, or we had lost when it was important that we should win. Everyone has times like that. I would be lying, for instance, if I told you that the 1995 World Cup was an enjoyable experience. But there was never a time when the simple act of going on to a rugby field, playing the game for my team and doing my best to outplay, outthink or outwit the opposition was not enjoyable. If rugby was not fun to play, we would not be bothering with it.

And it was never more fun than when I was playing for my school, Cwmtawe. I still have marvellous memories of those Saturday mornings on the rec at Pontardawe, next to Maybury's abattoir – some of the smells were fairly memorable as well. We had a lovely kit: royal blue with a grey stripe in the middle of two yellow bands. I always had the whitest shorts (my mother used to boil wash them) and the cleanest boots of anybody in the team. We'd get there at ten for a 10.30 start. After the match my mother would make us cawl – a traditional Welsh vegetable broth we always had on a Saturday – then we'd go off to watch Trebanos play in the afternoon. They were wonderful days. The rugby was good, but there was no pressure on you. You were encouraged to play the best rugby you could and to make the best of your skills, but there was no shouting or recriminations if you lost. We won more often than not anyway, and we enjoyed that, but it wasn't a matter of life and death. There's time enough to get worried about results later on in your rugby life.

Some of the best days were when we played local rivals like Ysgol Gyfun in Ystalyfera. Matches against them were our equivalent of Swansea v. Llanelli as they were also a Swansea Valley school and took many of their pupils from the same areas; quite often you'd be playing against boys from your own village, or boys you otherwise knew. There would always be a bit of a crowd as well.

We played roughly the same group of schools through the years, so I got used to playing against teams like Olchfa in Swansea, Ynysawdre from Bridgend and Gowerton. One of the games I remember best dates from my early days in the senior side. One of our first matches was against the Old Boys, who were normally made up of people who had left the school in the last two or three years, and I found myself playing against my brother Anthony, who had been the school and Wales Schools scrum-half the previous year. It was pretty competitive. Being such a close family possibly made it more so.

I don't know how much difference it would have made to my rugby life had I gone to another school – that's the sort of question you can't ever really answer – but I find it very hard to believe that anywhere else could have been better for me. Cwmtawe had a reputation as a good school producing a fair number of Wales Schools players and some who went on to distinguished first-class careers: Bleddyn Bowen and my brother Anthony, both a few years older than me, and, most famously, Gareth Edwards (Cwmtawe had previously been Pontardawe Grammar School, Edwards' old school). Nowadays, the buildings I went to school in are part of Neath College, consistently one of the strongest under-18 teams in Wales.

The headmaster, Dr John Griffiths, was rugby mad. There was never any difficulty in being flexible when it came to staff or pupils involved in rugby. He regarded it as an important part of school life, along with other sports such as cricket, basketball and athletics. For the masters involved in the game, it was a real labour of love. Gwyn Lewis was a major influence, particularly in the junior years. Gethin Edwards – Gareth's brother – was a teacher at Cwmtawe while I was there, and Bill Samuel, who had been Gareth's mentor, was still on the staff. Royston Davies, who had won a Wales Schools cap as a prop, had returned to Cwmtawe as a teacher after finishing college; he is now also coach of Trebanos. Most important for me, however, was Geoff (pronounced 'Joff') Davies, who was for me what Bill Samuel had been for Gareth Edwards. Throughout my career Geoff freely gave advice and guidance. Whenever I had a problem or a worry about the game, he was there; in time, he would always know to expect a phone call if I had been dropped by Wales. He is a determined man who enjoyed success in sevens competitions and against our local rivals, but he never put any pressure on us. If we lost, we lost; we just had to try to do better next time. There was no in-depth analysis of why we lost, no bawling out or shouting. It simply wasn't like that.

When I was in the under-15 team, we won the Rosslyn Park Sevens at Roehampton. I think it was the first time we had entered, and nobody expected a small school from the Swansea Valley to beat the best schools in England, places like Dulwich. We had an extremely quick wing called Mark Gittins, who also played for Wales Schools. He was never the most skilful of players, but we knew that if we managed to work him into space he would be away, and the chances were he would score. We went back a couple of times after that, but weren't so successful. I think the furthest we got was the quarter-final.

But I'd had some success in rugby even before I started going to Cwmtawe, having already played for West Wales under-11s in the annual match against East Wales. John Devereux was also in the side that day, and my outside-half was Sean McCarthy from Bridgend, now better known as a footballer for Swansea City, Oldham and quite a few other league teams. Later on my brother Rhodri played in the same fixture. His outside-half that day was Robert Howley, and Nick Beal, who has since played for England and the Lions but at that time lived in Haverfordwest, was also in the team.

From that age, my aim in life was to play rugby for my country. I made it at the age of fifteen. I remember Phil Bennett saying that the greatest feeling a player will ever have is the first time he plays for Wales, that nothing can ever quite match it. He was right; I clearly remember receiving my cap and my Wales Schools blazer badge with the feathers on it. It was the spring of 1981, and we played against the South of Scotland at Cardiff Arms Park. I was captain, and Stuart Davies, who became a team-mate for Swansea and Wales and a very good friend, was also in the team. We changed in the old Cardiff club dressing rooms. There were busloads of children from Cwmtawe at the ground, and all my family were there too. From the moment I ran out on to the Arms Park, our Mecca, my sole aim in life was to repeat the experience. That first appearance for the Schools side gave me all the inspiration I needed to drive myself on to full international level. Funnily enough, the one thing I can't remember about that game is the score. But I know we won.

The following year I was captain again for an under-16 game against England at Cardiff. There was one incident during this match that caused quite a stir at the time, and I've never seen anything like it before or since. The England outside-half missed a penalty kick, and the referee, Alyn Wyn Bevan, called for it to be taken again because the crowd had been booing. There was an announcement asking the crowd to refrain from booing, and the penalty was successfully converted the second time.

The year after that, 1983, this Welsh Schools side did the Grand Slam. The coaching at that time was handled by Huw Powell, John Huw Williams and John Elgar Williams – 'John Huw' and 'John Elgar' to us. We used to train up in the Amman Valley, where John Elgar was based, which suited me fine as it was close to home. The captain was Alun Carter, who was an incredibly good schoolboy player; indeed, quite a few of that team went on to play international rugby: Glyn Llewellyn was in the second row, Rowland Phillips played back row and Stuart Parfitt centre.

My outside-half for that campaign – Stephen Jones, always known as Steff – was from Cwmtawe as well. He came from Gwaen-cae-Gurwen, and lived a couple of doors down from Gareth Edwards. I remember watching him a year or so earlier playing outside my brother Ant in a match against Leicester Youth and thinking, the way you do when you see somebody who has something special, 'He's brilliant – he's got everything.' He was a fine goal-kicker, but his great strength as an outside-half was the way he went past his opponents. The other thing that was remarkable about him was that he loved tackling. He would literally push players out of the way to get at people and he'd always put his body on the line. It wasn't that he was that big either – only about five foot ten.

As a result, Steff had every club in the area chasing him, but for some reason his senior career never took off. He went to Neath and also played for Aberavon before spending four or five years at Swansea, as backup to Aled Williams. If you'd watched him play at the age of seventeen, you'd have bet on him being first choice not just for a senior club, but for Wales. You always wonder why some talents do not develop at senior level. Maybe Steff put a little too much emphasis on his tackling at the expense of the more creative parts of his game. He certainly seemed to lose confidence in his innate flair. And whereas I continued to be close to Geoff Davies, regularly ringing him for advice, Steff seemed to drift away a little. He certainly hasn't had a bad career, though. He's still involved at Cwmgors and made a good impression when he was player-coach at Vardre, and before that at Tenby United. He is now teaching at the Wern School, my opponents in my first ever school match. You can't help wondering what might have been, though.

And Steff wasn't the only player in this talented Schools side who didn't go on to do as much as was expected. In Alun

Carter, Rowland Phillips and Andy Coughlin from Newport, we had an excellent back row who scored most of our tries. While Carter and Phillips went on to good senior careers and Wales caps, Coughlin, who had looked a terrific player at that age, hardly played any senior rugby.

We travelled to France for the first fixture and got a result against a huge pack who looked like fully grown men to us. We went on to beat Scotland at Stradey, then Ireland, who always had good Schools sides, at Cork. The decider was played in April at Pontypridd, where England fielded a few players who went on to make names for themselves – Victor Ubogu at prop, Andy Blackmore at lock and Will Carling and Kevin Simms at centre. Two incidents stand out for me from this hard-fought game. The first was a drop goal by their scrum-half, Mark Hancock; the referee awarded it, but I'm not sure to this day that he hadn't really punted it. Then, right at the end of the game, I tackled Will Carling as he was about to score in the corner. It was a crucial tackle: had he scored, England would have won. As it was, Wales held on for a 13–12 win.

The year after that, when I was captain, we didn't play Ireland and lost to England, but we beat France and Scotland, who for some reason we played at home for the second year running – although playing in Wrexham felt to us as though we were going halfway there. There was yet another Jones from Cwmtawe in the team that year: Steven, better known as Spud, who played in the centre. Spud was another player you felt might go on to do more. He joined the Metropolitan Police and played for them. Later, he was at Vardre, and now he plays for Cwmtwrch. Swansea Valley boys don't seem to move very far, and when they do, it does not seem to be for long!

So Schools rugby was pretty strong when I started out, and my impression is that youth rugby is still in reasonably good shape in Wales. When you visit clubs there are a lot of youngsters who obviously love the game and enjoy playing. When I walk around Trebanos I bump into children who tell me how they scored a try last week or how their team has been doing, and they are obviously getting a lot out of the experience. International results have certainly been better than at senior level. We might not win all the time, but there haven't been the terrible hammerings the senior team has taken at times.

Even so, there are problems. Schools are under immense pressure to produce the best possible examination results. We didn't have league tables back in the early 1980s and inspections were much less frequent. Inevitably staff have had to place greater emphasis on academic success. Sport and physical education are a part of the national curriculum, but only a small part, and there is much else to be fitted in as well. All of this has put a lot more pressure on teachers. After the disputes of the 1980s, many decided that they would do the hours and carry out the duties stipulated in their contract and no more. Activities like rugby, which relied on teachers taking the attitude of my teachers at Cwmtawe, who gave up their time on Wednesday afternoons and Saturday mornings, lost out badly.

The social context has changed as well. Nowadays, children have a much greater range of possible activities open to them. I reckon I spent ninety per cent of my free time outside (or inside if the weather was bad) playing sport; today's children not only have a much greater number of television programmes trying to grab their attention, there's also the pull of computer games and the Internet. Our climate doesn't help in this. The fact that it is much less likely to be cold, wet and unpleasant out in Australia, South Africa and some parts of New Zealand is at least part of the reason why our children are more likely to be found in front of a television or computer screen than outside throwing or kicking a ball around.

We have to accept that rugby can no longer hope to enjoy the position it once had in many schools in Wales, unchallenged as the main winter sport, getting most of the energy, resources and attention. It now has to compete against a wider range of sports and activities, and suffers from the pressures on schools I have already mentioned. But I have no objection to this spread of activity. I have always loved rugby and I'll be delighted if my children do too, but I want them to have the opportunity to take part in as many games and activities as they can, to find the ones that they genuinely love. Rugby has to work for its position.

I think the game did get a little complacent in the 1970s and 1980s, perhaps even as late as the early 1990s. It was assumed that the flow of talent from the schools would continue, come what may. I was very concerned a few years ago to find that Cwmtawe, which could put out three senior sides when I was a pupil, was struggling to field one. Reorganisation is an element in this decline – there is no longer a sixth form at Cwmtawe; pupils of that age move on to Neath College – but the general lack of curricular and extra-curricular activities has played its part too.

A fightback has begun. The Welsh Rugby Union's Dragons Rugby Trust, with which I have a very strong connection, is working on the creation of a network of local development officers. The idea is that every school should have someone to turn to for advice and guidance on the game. In time, the hope is that there will be around 200 of them, one for every secondary school, sixth form or tertiary college in Wales, each one also attached to a club and a group of primary schools. The trust is some way off from actually accomplishing this, but a strong start has been made. The Lloyds TSB League, which has just started its fourth season, has also been a great success in reintroducing regular Saturday morning rugby, and the membership has expanded consistently.

The emphasis throughout all this is on children enjoying their rugby. This matters more than anything at every level of play. The elite group we want to see going on to play first-class and international rugby should be given every encouragement and assistance. But it isn't just about elites. If we cater only to a small group, we will make no progress. It is vital for the future of rugby that you encourage people who aren't part of the athletic elite. You don't have to be capable of playing for Swansea or Neath to make an important contribution to the game. One reason why the Welsh game has been strong is that we have a dense network of clubs like Trebanos, playing at their own level – Trebanos are currently in Division Five West – any one of which may find or encourage the next great Welsh player. Those clubs need players, officials, referees and supporters. The best way of ensuring that they get them is to make sure that children's early experience of rugby is happy and enjoyable.

I am not sure we are achieving this at the moment. It is good that there are lots of youngsters playing the game – all children should be encouraged to play team sports because team activities encourage the development of social skills, communication and the ability to work with other people – but too much pressure is being placed on them too young. It worries me when I hear of eight- and nine-year-olds playing in competitions; it depresses me when I visit clubs' junior sections to hear talk of building winning teams and maintaining unbeaten records. At that age the emphasis should be entirely on enjoying the game and building a few skills. These kids are too young to be getting competitive – the emphasis is all wrong.

More clubs need to have the attitude of Cefn Cribwr, where the aim is to give all the youngsters a game and let them enjoy it. They do play in competitions, but I am always struck that the emphasis of Mike Kelly and Nigel Coleman's coaching is entirely on enjoyment. If there are twenty lads there, they will all get a game; it isn't a matter of picking the best side, even for local derbies against Pyle and Kenfig Hill. The club's aim is to give as large a number of youngsters as possible a sense of the fun that can be had from the game.

Too much competition too young is, of course, not a new problem – in the same *Rothmans Rugby Union Yearbook* that has the details of Wales Schools' Grand Slam, there is an article by Steve Jones, the editor, in which he complains about the same attitudes I have been talking about. He wrote:

'There are too many tournaments, too much silverware at stake, too much celebration of the winners and not enough emphasis on the fun of mere participation . . . Let enjoyment be the be-all and end-all, and teach the boys to enjoy themselves in defeat. Above all, teach no set moves other than to pass the ball or run with it.' Those are exactly my views, and I think the problem has become worse. I don't believe the people who say that competition early on is the way to produce people who will be winners as adults; in my view such an approach is far more likely to turn young players off rugby. If your aim as a coach with eight- or nine-year-olds is simply to produce a winning side, the chances are that you will concentrate on the better players rather than develop the skills of the entire group. At that age you should be finding out about the game, discovering what you can do – not being told what you can't do. There is plenty of time to start being competitive in your early teens, when life starts to get competitive anyway.

Another serious problem is the number of games in which our young players are taking part. You get youngsters who are playing for a school, a district and the youth section of a club side. Graham Henry has talked about one youngster he met who had played 93 games that year, a ludicrous number. That is an extreme case, but fifty or sixty is not that unusual. Such experiences have their physical consequences, like prop forwards of 21 and 22 complaining about neck problems, but the more damaging and widespread problems are mental – young men who have played a lifetime's worth of competitive rugby by the time they are twenty and are mentally tired of the game at a time when they should be bringing freshness and enthusiasm to the professional game.

There is no easy answer to this problem. The same people will always be in demand for school, district and club sides. The natural reaction of the youngster who is an enthusiast and is good at the game is to say 'I enjoy it' and be quite happy to take on as many games as he can play. You can't stop him doing it – it is not as if he is contracted to anyone.

It is a matter of common sense and a sense of responsibility from everyone involved – parents, teachers and coaches. The example that should be held out to them is the limit the Welsh Rugby Union places on the young players they have under contract, the sixty members of their national elite 16–21 squad. They are told that they are not to play more than one game in a week, that if they find themselves under pressure to take part in more then they should contact the union, which will give a very firm no on their behalf. What is good for the elite squads, in order to safeguard their long-term fitness and enthusiasm for the game, should be good enough for every other young player in Wales.

We should also be wary of identifying and isolating talent too early. It should not be too hard to spot the young players who are most gifted – they are not necessarily the biggest, strongest or quickest, but those who have the ability to beat people and to make instinctive decisions, those who have footballing talent. One of the things coaches have to recognise is that you can't teach an instinctive talent for rugby, but you can identify it and provide the environment in which it can best be nurtured. There is a temptation to try to define that elite group early, but this should be resisted. Good development officers should be aware of any outstanding twelve- or thirteen-year-olds in their area, and keep an eye on them. Of course you don't want to lose talented young players, but you want to keep them in their own environment at that age. Taking someone out at the age of twelve and defining him as a member of an elite is only likely to isolate him and make him a target – both ways of losing him. Fourteen or fifteen, when national squads are first being selected, is early enough.

The vital thing at this stage is to encourage players to develop their individual skills. My father knew how important this was. From an early age, whenever we were out kicking a ball, he'd encourage me to practise kicking with my left foot. If I kicked one with my right, he'd say, 'Right, now kick the next one with your left.' There was no pressure on me. I did it because I wanted to do it, and it meant that when I came into senior rugby I could kick equally well and comfortably with either foot. I carried on practising, kicking alternately with either foot, all the way through my career.

There is nothing better for developing skills than playing sevens. Local sevens tournaments – village competitions staged as part of a carnival week – were the first competitive rugby I played. In terms of developing instinctive football skills, sevens is almost certainly better than the fifteen-a-side game. You can't look at five or six set moves, or say, 'If it rains, we'll have to keep it tight.' There is no hiding place, you have to live off your skills and wits. You have to learn how to pass, how to beat a man or outwit a defence, and you have the space in which to do it. You also learn how to tackle. I used to play as the 'sweeper' in sevens teams and learned that tackling was a matter of technique, not power. You don't try to take someone much bigger than you head on and try to throw him back, but take him down as quickly as possible. You also find that if you use the proper technique and commit yourself to the tackle you are much less likely to get hurt; half-hearted challenges are far more likely to lead to injury because you tend to bounce off the man you are trying to stop.

I don't think it is a fluke that Scotland, where sevens is still taken seriously and the Melrose Sevens is one of the big events of the season, has a tradition of producing players, including forwards, with good all-round footballing skills. Their natural talents are sharpened for the fifteen-a-side game by playing sevens regularly and coping with the demands it makes on your skills.

Young players should also be encouraged to try out a variety of positions, even though physique and speed are always likely to label you. For instance, I was never likely to be anything other than a half-back, while there are others whose build means they are likely to play in the front row or on the wing. Eventually, of course, a decision has to be made, especially when it comes to the specialised positions, but a gifted player can switch between most of the other positions in the back division: Steve Jones has already played three different positions for Wales, Mike Catt has been just about everywhere from 10 to 15 for England and most of the top Australians – Burke, Larkham, Horan and others – have played international rugby in more than one position. Scrum-half is a little different. It is a position you have to learn. Someone like Austin Healey, who has moved between the wing and scrum-half, is an exception, but even then he took some time to adjust, and most of his caps in the last few years have come on the wing.

But there's no need to tie a young player down to a speciality too early. Playing a variety of positions is a good way of developing a range of skills and a vision of the game as a whole. I played more games at full-back for Swansea Valley under-15s because we had better cover at scrum-half; it wasn't exactly that I was looking for extra experience, but it certainly did me no harm. I later played a few games for Swansea at centre.

Nor do you want youngsters to be playing only rugby. That is one way to get bored with the game. You need other outlets. As well as playing too much, our young players play for too long during the year. We don't need competitions starting in August and a season which certainly feels as though it lasts all year. Six months is long enough, allowing them to play other sports like cricket during the rest of the year. Personally, I got a huge amount out of playing cricket, which was my other main game. In fact, my first caps for Wales were for cricket rather than rugby (there were cricket teams at under-11 and under-13 levels, while the youngest rugby team was at under-15 level). One of my under-11 team-mates was Anthony Cottey, who has been a successful county player for Glamorgan and Sussex and also an excellent footballer who played a few times for Swansea City, although I must admit that I chiefly remember him for being one of those rare team-mates who was smaller than I was!

I quite often get asked whether I think I could have made it as a professional cricketer. It is extremely hard to tell if you haven't tried, and once I had won my first rugby cap at the age of fifteen there was never any doubt where my commitment was going to be. I did not develop much as a cricketer between the ages of fifteen and eighteen simply because I did not work very hard at it. My commitment was to rugby, so that was the game I was most likely to succeed in. There were others who trod different paths. When I played rugby for Wales Students as a sixth-former, the outside-half was Hugh Morris, who later captained Glamorgan at cricket for years, opened the batting for England and is now a senior official with the England and Wales Cricket Board. Hugh was at the South Glamorgan Institute and played a fair amount of senior club rugby. He was a very talented footballer who might have made an extremely good rugby player, but in the same way that I chose rugby, Hugh's great love was cricket.

But cricket gave me an outlet, a sporting activity which took me away from rugby for a few months and gave me a different focus. It was good insurance against getting stale. I was mainly a batsman, but I enjoyed fielding and bowled medium-pace for school teams, although I was never regarded as an all-rounder at representative level. I have no doubt at all that it was also a practical help to my rugby, as it probably was for Robert Howley, also a Wales Schools cricketer, and Colin Stephens, who played for the Wales senior cricket team. Jonathan Griffith was close to senior county standard and Geraint Lewis and my brother Rhodri are also very good cricketers.

As a batsman you need to be able to react quickly, to make swift decisions and use hand-eye coordination. It is all short, sharp work – particularly when somebody like Greg Thomas is trying to bounce you – and helps to develop natural ball skills. Another important skill batsmanship has in common with the art of the scrum-half is footwork. It is crucial that both get their feet in the right place; in fact, there is nothing more important to a scrum-half's game. I tell the young scrum-halves I work with that when you are clearing the ball from a ruck or maul you need to anticipate, a yard or two beforehand, where the ball will come out and how you will get it away. The key to getting that right is having your feet in the right place. If they are not, you will not get the ball away as quickly as you should and the pass is likely to be forced or thrown too hard. However quick your hands are, if the position of your feet is wrong you won't provide a smooth service.

The 'other sport' does not have to be cricket, of course. I also got a lot out of playing basketball (although it was never my favourite game) and squash at school. Short, sharp, reactive work of the kind both these sports require is good for a scrum-half, or any other rugby player. Ball games develop your skills and your hand-eye coordination, making you more of a natural ball player.

If these suggestions are followed, it is my opinion that Wales will have a steady flow of young people leaving its schools who are well-equipped for the challenges of the professional game. As I have already said, I think the schools and youth game are in reasonably good shape. The real problems appear to be starting at the next stage up, and seem to have become more acute since the game became professional. Getting that transition into the professional game right for the players in the 16–21 age group is absolutely essential if Wales is to become a leading rugby nation again.

# **4** Breaking In

'As a young player, I knew that I was always going to have to work as well as play rugby. If I ever had any doubts on that score, they were ended during my first few weeks at Swansea. I'd arrive for training and see people like David Richards and Malcolm Dacey turning up in their suits, straight from work. It was a valuable reminder that even the best players had to work for their living. At the same time, the fact that they managed to develop professional careers as well as play rugby to such a high level inspired a desire in me to do the same.'

W HEN I WAS READY FOR THE MOVE into senior club rugby, the process and the progression were remarkably simple. You were almost certain to go to your local club, which in my case meant Swansea or Neath. It was just a matter of being spotted by them, receiving an invitation to training and hoping that they were sufficiently impressed to register you and give you a few games.

In my case, I was watched while playing for West Glamorgan Schools in a representative match at Olchfa School in Swansea by a man named Gethin Thomas, who was involved in the Swansea set-up as forwards coach. He invited me along to training, so I soon found myself as an awestruck schoolboy in the same changing room as people I had idolised from the terraces at St Helen's, top-class international players like David Richards, Malcolm Dacey and Richard Moriarty. When the club decided that they wanted me to join them as a player, it was a simple matter of signing a registration form – which I did, in October 1983. That was the only formal relationship I had with the club: a registration which was renewed every season.

When the All Whites did ask me to join them, it was one of the easiest decisions I have ever made. They were the only club I had ever really wanted to play for. My father had played a few games for Neath so there was always a possible connection with them, and I was invited to join them not long after I got into the Swansea team. Brian Thomas wanted me to play alongside Jonathan Davies. You always have a think about an offer like that, but I was never going to accept it. Swansea had always been my club.

The modern player of sixteen, seventeen or eighteen years of age finds himself in a much more complicated world. The most talented players in that age group have been in the Welsh Rugby Union's national elite squad, those sixty players who are regarded as potential future internationals and receive funding to help with training and education (I know of a couple who have used theirs to help with school bursaries). The reputation of those young players, and anyone else in the age group who has played representative rugby, is far greater than I ever enjoyed at the same age. They are known not only to every major club in Wales, but to quite a few of the English clubs too. From the age of fifteen or sixteen they will have been receiving calls from those clubs. Some of them will already have agents.

Why? Because the stakes are a great deal higher. The question facing me was a simple one: which club did I want to play for? Swansea worked out very well for me. I believe that I would have played my entire career with them had it not been for the shift to professionalism. But had things not worked out I would just have gone back to Trebanos and hoped for an offer to play for Neath or some other club. Today's young player has a potentially career-defining decision to make. Rugby can be a very lucrative career. Money is, of course, a major factor in any decision made by these young players and their parents. But there are other factors that must come into the decision, above all their correct development as players and as people. The biggest offer in terms of money will not always be the best one in the long term.

As a young player, I knew that I was always going to have to work as well as play rugby. If I ever had any doubts on that score, they were ended during my first few weeks at Swansea. I'd arrive for training and see people like David Richards and Malcolm Dacey turning up in their suits, straight from work. It was a valuable reminder that even the best players had to work for their living. At the same time, the fact that they managed to develop professional careers as well as play rugby to such a high level inspired a desire in me to do the same.

Today's young player has the chance to build a life exclusively around rugby. A good professional contract means he has no need to look for work elsewhere. That might seem like a good thing to someone whose only desire in life is to play rugby to the highest level possible. It would probably have looked good to me the best part of a couple of decades ago. But there is a trap in this as well. Any professional sport is a high-risk career. You may get injured, lose form or your place to a better player – or one whose style is supposed to fit the team better. Even if your career is an extremely successful one, playing rugby will not last you a lifetime. You can also become too narrowly focused. A player who only has rugby in his life is much more likely to become bored or stale than someone who has other outlets and activities.

Good advice is important all the way through your career. I was always lucky in this. My parents have always supported me, and I have always been able to turn to Geoff Davies. Having good people around you is never more important than when you are making the transition from school to senior rugby. Enormously important decisions have to be made, and you have little experience on which to base those decisions. Of course, the best advice will not necessarily guarantee that you will make the right decisions. My own experience as a sixth-former is an example of that. Sometimes when I talk to young players I use my own experiences to provide positive examples they might follow or ideas they might try, but this was a real case of 'don't do as I did, do as I say'.

I did not set out to fail my examinations. I wanted to go to college and had my sights set on the South Glamorgan Institute at Cyncoed in Cardiff (nowadays UWIC). It was the place where you wanted to go if you were a good rugby player. John Devereux, who won his first cap on the same day as me, was a student there. But at the time I was totally focused on my rugby, which was going very well. I got into the Wales Schools team and then, while I was still at school, I started playing for Swansea. Life could not have been better, and I stopped paying enough attention to my schoolwork. Mentally I was elsewhere. It was, I have to admit, entirely my fault. I had Geoff, my mother and father and all my family saying 'You've got to get your exams!' I couldn't have had better advice and support. The All Whites went on a tour of Barbados in May 1984, not long before I took the exams. Naturally I didn't want to miss that and I promised my parents that I'd take my books and do plenty of study. Well, I did take my books with me, but I would be lying if I said they got a lot of attention.

I went back to school a year later to try to get my qualifications, but it did not work. I was too firmly focused on playing for Swansea. Everything was going very well for me and, to be honest, by that stage I didn't really want to go to college. Going to Cyncoed would have meant playing my rugby there, which would have got in the way of playing for Swansea. I just wanted to go on enjoying my rugby at Swansea, especially since people were already starting to talk about me playing for Wales. I was hoping that somebody at Swansea would find me a job. I gave out the right signals, and Mike James found me work with John Morse, a firm of solicitors.

Of course things did not work out badly for me. I did play for Wales, when I was only just twenty. Had I gone to college it might not have happened as quickly. I had a long career as an international rugby player and the contacts I made during that career have helped me to develop work outside rugby. But things might have been very different had I been injured or dropped down the pecking order for Swansea or Wales. My prospects would have been pretty limited. Not having gone to college is a genuine regret. Ninety per cent of the people I meet or do business with nowadays have been to college. I haven't, and I feel that I have missed out on a worthwhile experience.

As that story shows, you can't make people be sensible or force them to take the right options, but you can ensure that they get the best possible advice. This is one area where I think Welsh rugby and the Welsh Rugby Union are getting a great deal right, through the work of the Dragons Rugby Trust, mentioned in the last chapter, the charitable body set up by the union to ensure that a development process is in place for junior players. It is overseen by Terry Cobner, while major figures from the WRU like Glanmor Griffiths, Vernon Pugh, Derek Quinnell and Dennis Hughes are trustees of the charity. It has a deliberately small staff – only three or four people: Arthur Jones, the manager, and Ceri Thomas, the project manager, supported by a couple of administrative staff (Anthony Clement also works part-time running their Chwarae Teg scheme which promotes the game in schools and under which there is a monthly fair play award to a player or club) – in order to reduce overheads and ensure that as much money as possible goes into the development of young players. Part of the trust's function is finding sponsorship for junior rugby and the people involved in it; thus, British Telecom provide development officers with vehicles and are now equipping them with mobile phones, Lloyds TSB support schools and youth leagues, and there is also support from companies like Zurich and Reebok. About the only thing the DRT don't do exceptionally well is publicise their activities. I am sure if more people knew about the work they are doing, greater support would come in.

An excellent example of this good work is the dedicated industry of Alun Davies, the ACE (Athlete Career and Education) adviser who works with members of the elite national squad. Alun is a former Maesteg scrum-half – I played against him several times in my early years at Swansea and always found him a tough, extremely physical opponent – a Welsh-speaker from Banwen. He has been trained in the ACE programme, which is designed to assist elite athletes in the management of their lives, and is the only ACE-licensed adviser appointed by any rugby union. The appointment is funded by the Sports Council of Wales and the Dragons Rugby Trust, and I think it says a great deal for the foresight of Terry Cobner and the trust that they backed this initiative.

The elite squad meets six to eight times a year to go through a series of sessions. No more than about half of these will be on the field. The rest are classroom sessions led by Alun which provide advice on all aspects of rugby career development. He also has a regular programme of meetings with the elite squad members and their parents with the aim of guiding them towards the best possible future. A key part of this is discussing education and then setting up links with colleges and universities, in particular working out ways in which they can be flexible in accommodating players who want to study. The good news is that most colleges, universities and even employers are keen to be flexible, to help young players combine different elements in their lives.

Mixing top-class rugby and studies, however, can be tough, particularly if your rugby career progresses rapidly. A good current example is Rhys Williams. He got into the senior World Cup squad only a few months after playing in the under-19 competition, won his first cap against Ireland at the end of the 2000 Six Nations and has been in the team virtually the whole time since. Rhys found it extremely difficult to balance his university course with the demands of playing for Cardiff and Wales, so he wasn't doing too well in his studies and dropped out. A bit of flexibility was needed on both sides, and Alun has been working with Rhys and his college to find a way of getting him back to complete his course. Rhys is still only 21 and is a gifted player who could be on the threshold of a long international career. He might not need his degree for a long time, but it will ensure he has prospects and options outside the game when he finishes playing. There are more jobs in the game than there were in the amateur days, but not enough for everybody.

My own work for the Dragons Rugby Trust also focuses on helping players in the elite squad. Towards the end of my playing career I got into discussions with Reebok about possible ways of helping youth rugby. One of the things I was most aware of throughout my rugby career was how lucky I was to have the advice of Geoff Davies, and that many players did not have this advantage. You can always look to your immediate family for support, and I could not have been luckier in this respect either, but members of your close family go through the same ups and downs as you do. I find this now when I watch my brother Rhodri playing for Swansea. Like my parents, I am desperate for him to do well and I feel his suffering when he is not playing well or is not selected for important games. It is hard for me to be objective about him.

Everyone needs someone outside the family to talk to about worries and problems, even if only to put them in perspective. Geoff always did this for me, he does it for Rhod and I know he has been very important to Robert Howley. Often during my career I was worried about something and would try to think it out by myself, but would only get it put properly into perspective after I had spoken to Geoff. He was particularly important during the times when my confidence was low. This didn't mean he would always tell me I was right about something – far from it. He could be quite critical, but he was always constructive, and was always at his best when it came to helping me deal with adverse criticism. This is perhaps the toughest aspect of life in top-class rugby and the hardest to deal with. You can be criticised by the media and by fans, and it may be totally unfair. The worst thing about it is the effect it has on your family and friends. But it is part and parcel of the game, and you have to learn to live with it.

I wanted all young players to have the advantage of a mentor who could do for them what Geoff did for me. The idea I came up with, and which I put to Terry Cobner and John Bevan at the Welsh Rugby Union along with Gareth Davies from Reebok, was to introduce a mentoring scheme for members of the elite national squads. Some people would doubtless say that you should not need mentoring, that the players who do need it are probably not tough enough to handle top-class rugby. The answer to that is a simple one: look at the benefits Gareth Edwards derived throughout his career from his association with Bill Samuel. If the greatest rugby player any of us can remember found a mentor useful, then surely it could prove valuable to other players as well. An example of a current player who would surely benefit is Arwel Thomas. He gets a lot of moral support from friends and the community in Trebanos, but there is nobody doing for him what Geoff did for me and Bill did for Gareth.

I work with the four scrum-halves in the national elite squad: Rhodri Wells, who comes from Skewen, goes to Christ's College and plays for the Wales Schools side; Rhodri Jones (no relation), who goes to Usk College and is a member of the under-19 squad; and two boys from Ysgol Llanhari, the Welsh-language school near Bridgend that Scott Gibbs and Matthew Back went to. Alyn Lake is also in the under-19 squad, while Simon Cole is a couple of years younger, but has already been identified as a potential international player.

Part of the idea is to help them with their rugby. I try to watch them play regularly, and when we meet part of the time will be devoted to skills work – kicking a ball or some drills so I can see how their skills are progressing. I always ask them about how they think their recent games went, how they feel about them. I may find that they feel they have a problem with some aspect of the game, or possibly with the way they are being asked to play for a particular team. We discuss the problem, and if necessary I may talk to the teacher or coach concerned so we can work out a solution which keeps everyone happy.

But it is not all about rugby. The question I always ask fairly early in the meeting is 'How's it going?', and by that I don't just mean in rugby terms. They may have worries about school or at home which have nothing to do with rugby but which can still affect their development as players and as people. The idea is that I should provide a sympathetic but independent ear, a shoulder to cry on if they need one. There might also be questions about their lifestyle. There are all sorts of potential distractions for young men in their late teens and you want to keep them on the straight and narrow while recognising that the last thing you should be telling them to do is go to school, play rugby and nothing else. They need a balance in their lives. I would certainly worry if they were out drinking with their friends every night, but there is a time and place for that and for other things people in their age group enjoy.

The aim is to help these young players reach their potential, to encourage them in their ambitions to play for Wales and the Lions, to be the best in the world. This does involve sacrifices – staying in when friends are out, being extremely careful about what you eat and drink – but it can be achieved by somebody who has a balanced, varied lifestyle. I don't remember many monks making it to the top in rugby. In order to help them to the best of my ability, I am available to them 24 hours a day. I always tell them to ring me if there's anything they want to talk about.

A good relationship, of course, takes a while to develop. As a youngster it can take you time to build up the confidence needed to deal with an older person as a friend. When I first joined Swansea I said very little in the first few weeks and it was a long time before I felt I could speak to people like Dai Richards and Malcolm Dacey as anything approaching equals. But it is worth persevering. Mostyn Richards, the development manager at the WRU, is keen for the project to last three or four years. There is little point in starting up, then just walking away after a year. Three to four years would be long enough to build up a strong relationship, one which might go on to last through the player's career and provide the union, Reebok and the DRT with solid feedback in terms of how well the scheme had worked.

Things are still on a very limited scale. David Young is working with the prop forwards in the elite squad, but there is as yet no funding for other positions. In time, we would like to extend the programme so that it covers every position and every player in the elite squad. Money, of course, is an issue. You do have to provide some financial compensation for the time involved in mentoring. It is not a vast amount, but I know that I could not afford to do it without some payment.

There is also the question of finding the right people to do it. There are obvious advantages in using players whose careers were recent, who would have been watched by the young players. You will always take seriously advice from someone you idolised as a child. But they also need to be able to make a commitment to the mentoring and to the young people involved. There would be obvious benefits, for instance, in getting someone like Neil Jenkins involved now as a mentor to the next generation of Welsh outside-halves. They will have grown up watching Neil play, watching him score a record number of points for Wales and could only benefit from the example of his unmatched professionalism, deep thought on the game and experience of the pressures and problems of top-class rugby. If anybody knows about coping with criticism and coming out ahead of the game, it's Neil.

Mentoring is a positive means by which former players can put something back into the game that has rewarded them. Not everybody wants to become a coach or a media pundit. One of the things we have been rather bad at in Wales is making constructive use of the expertise and knowledge of former players. I look, for instance, at the way in which someone like Bleddyn Bowen, who has a deep knowledge of the game and could contribute a great deal, has been allowed to drift away. Nowadays he is far more likely to be found on the golf course than on a rugby ground, and this is a real loss to the game in Wales.

Mentors complement the work of the ACE adviser in the same way that the DRT, the WRU, the Sports Council of Wales and the clubs must regard each other as partners in the work of doing our best for young Welsh players. The union already puts a great deal of money into the DRT, funding which needs to be maintained and if at all possible increased. It would also be good to see Graham Henry taking a more active part in the work of the DRT. He has always been happy to endorse it and attend events, but a truly active input from him, using his experience not just as national coach but as a successful headteacher, would be extremely valuable. From his comments about the importance of ensuring that players have more than just rugby in their lives, we know that he is strongly in favour of the trust's objectives, while the appointment of Nigel Walker as development adviser to the national squad shows that he is aware of the value of Alun Davies's work with younger players.

Before clubs sign a young player I would like to see them sitting down with him, his parents and the ACE adviser (if he is one of the national elite squad) or the district development officer (if he is not) and discussing all aspects of his development. How much money the club is prepared to offer is obviously important, but it must not be the sole consideration. The club should be offering a package which will not only advance his rugby, but his all-round development. And promises made at that meeting must be kept. Again, it is also up to the player to take some responsibility. You can't make a youngster who is only interested in rugby and is convinced he will play for Wales take his education seriously any more than Geoff and my parents, for all their efforts, were able to make me see sense over my A levels. But the club can ensure that a decent range of opportunities is on offer, and do its best to make sure that its youngsters make the most of them.

There is no doubt the range of opportunities and qualifications is wider than it was. Players on club apprenticeship schemes can now take an NVQ qualification in rugby studies, something they can put on their CVs and use towards getting on to college courses. There are programmes like the diploma in rugby studies offered by Carmarthenshire College in Llanelli, or the sports studies degrees at UWIC. One of the most satisfying aspects of the work I do with young players is in partnership with Jim Houlihan of Sportrain Wales, which has been appointed by the DRT to supervise club apprenticeship schemes for young players. We work together to promote apprenticeships and to find employers like ntl and HSBC who are prepared to offer flexible work which can be fitted around a rugby career.

It is inevitable that rugby people will tend to look for jobs around the game, in coaching, development work, marketing or media. Professionalism has certainly created a range of jobs that were not there before, but it is still possible, and perhaps desirable, to have work outside the game. Mark Taylor is a good example of this. He works one day a week as an accountant for a garage in Llanelli. I have no doubt it gives him a change of focus and a worthwhile rest from rugby. It clearly does no harm to his game. It has not stopped him from becoming one of the best centres in the British Isles or the captain of Wales when David Young was injured. In fact, I would argue that it has probably helped him. He certainly has few worries to plague him about what he will do when he finishes playing. His experience and profile should make him a very attractive proposition for some employer. Of course, Mark started playing before the game was professional so he had to look for an alternative way of making a living, but he has seen no reason to stop work since. Some people might see this as an oddity, a hangover from the days of amateurism, but I would argue that it is a positive example to today's young players of somebody who has a life outside rugby and future prospects that are not completely dependent on the game.

# **5** Amateur Days

'I would not have developed as quickly as I did had Swansea not put their faith in me at an early age. They had done the same with Paul Moriarty and Aled Williams, both of whom were a year or so older than me, and would do so a few years later when Tony Clement, Richard Webster and Dai Young emerged from an extraordinarily good crop of youth players. At other clubs, Neil Jenkins, Scott Gibbs, John Devereux and Jonathan Davies all progressed rapidly into first-class and international rugby.'

THROUGHOUT MY CAREER, people have always thought I was older than I really was. Perhaps the reason was that I started early and played for a long time. There were sixteen and a half years between my debut in senior club rugby – against South Wales Police in November 1983, two weeks after my eighteenth birthday – and my last game, against Edinburgh in April 2000. On both occasions I was playing for Swansea at St Helen's. And, remarkably enough, my opponent at scrum-half in 1983, Nigel Whitehouse, refereed that match in 2000.

Those seventeen seasons did more than take me from my teens to my mid-thirties. They changed club rugby almost beyond recognition. In 1983 the game was amateur and the only competition the All Whites played in was the Welsh Cup. The rest were friendlies. We played 51 matches in my first season against opposition including Moseley, Harlequins, Halifax, Maesteg, Blackheath, London Welsh, South Glamorgan Institute and the Barbarians.

While nothing can match the importance of my family and my home village of Trebanos, other communities have been very important in my life. None more so than the All Whites, my club for fourteen of the seventeen seasons in which I played senior rugby. That sense of community was particularly important at the start, when I arrived at the club as an awestruck teenager who hardly said a word unless spoken to. I remember how tense I felt before my first training session, before going down to the ground with my father after a school day. It felt like the build-up to an international match, but the players made it so easy and comfortable for me.

The warmth of their welcome and the way I was looked after was typified by Huw Davies, always known as 'Spider', who was the first-team scrum-half at the time. He had been at the club for years and was at scrum-half when the All Whites won the Welsh Cup in 1978. I had great respect for him. He was small and quick, not the greatest passer in the world, but a very busy player. I had met him before joining the All Whites as he used to teach at Olchfa School in Swansea, one of our regular opponents at Cwmtawe. He was well into his thirties at the time – the club history refers to him being '28 plus VAT' – and coming to the end of his career, so he might have treated me as a threat. After all, I was after his place in the team. Instead, he took me under his wing and encouraged me, which was typical of the warmth of the atmosphere at Swansea. I played about ten matches in that first season, including the cup tie against Cardiff. He must have been disappointed to be left out of the biggest game of the season in favour of a youngster who had only been around for a few months, but he could not have been more helpful. Before the match he said to me, 'Good luck. You've got a great future in this game. Now go out and prove it.'

Spider also introduced me to some of the dodges you could use in training. Like any youngster trying to make his mark, I was always keen to be at the front when we were running during sessions. On one occasion he grabbed me from behind and said, 'Stop going so fast! You're showing me up, and I'm an old man now!' He became a very good friend, and years later would become my boss, appointing me as business development executive at the Swansea Building Society when he was chief executive. I have to wonder whether a modern player would be treated as well under the same circumstances. In 1983 I was only a threat to Spider's first-team place; nowadays I would be a threat to his very livelihood as a professional rugby player. Where he and other senior players saw me as the naïve schoolboy I was and looked after

me, I suspect the current attitude would be: 'He's a professional – he can look after himself.'

There were other people whose names never got into the
papers, but who made me feel just as welcome and played a
vital part in creating the atmosphere at St Helen's. There
was Colin Maxworthy, always known as Maxie, who looked
after the kit and was always the first person there, opening
the doors, checking the kit and laying it out. And John the
Dead, so-called because he worked as an undertaker. He used
to help with the rub-downs, and was extremely good at it
because he was a trained embalmer. Both of them had been
at the club for years, as had Bernard Cajot, who gave more
than fifty years of service to the Whites and was known and
liked by generations of players. He had played for and
coached the Athletic XV and he had even played scrum-half
for Trebanos alongside my father. My father remembered
him well, and Bernard never stopped reminding me about
it. Bernard was very quiet, the complete opposite of out-
spoken, but he was extremely knowledgeable about rugby
and always ready with a supportive word. He was always
good to me, and has been good to Rhodri as well. He loved
being a part of the Whites and he was always around on
training nights, filling bottles, helping with the rub-downs
and doing anything else he could to help. People talk about
giving loyal service to a club. I can't imagine that anyone has
ever given more loyal service and asked for less in return
than Bernard Cajot.

The squad were not all from Swansea – we had an England
international, Tony Swift, who would soon be joined by
another, Maurice Colclough, plus people like Mike Ruddock
from the Gwent Valleys – but we were essentially local boys
playing for our local club in front of local people. Nearly
everybody had been drawn from a thirty- to forty-mile radius.
Many of the senior players came from the same sort of
community as me, had come to the club via similar routes
and knew from their own experiences what it was like for me
to be making my way with the All Whites. Modern squads are

drawn from a far wider catchment area, so the experience is inevitably slightly different today.

We trained together twice a week. Modern professional outfits often have two sessions in a day, but it would be difficult to be more professional in outlook than people like David Richards, Mark Davies, Gareth Roberts and Roger Blyth. They were highly committed and hugely competitive, and certainly were not going to give an inch to a teenager who had just come into the squad. They would always put in extra time to work on their fitness and their skills – which meant training at lunchtime or at night after they had finished work. There was none of the obligation which goes hand in hand with professionalism, but they knew that a couple of training sessions a week were not sufficient to develop the skills and fitness levels they required to reach their full potential. If you were ambitious, you went out and trained by yourself or with friends, hoping that this would give you the edge on your rivals. I used to go to the park in Trebanos with a couple of friends and half a dozen rugby balls and we'd practise goalkicking and tactical kicking. It built up commitment and dedication and made me, and them, better players. It was never a chore because I enjoyed doing it.

Swansea was a strong team. They had won the Welsh Merit Table and the *Western Mail* Championship – the nearest thing we had to a competition apart from the cup – the season before. The cornerstone of the front row was Clive Williams, always known for some reason as 'Scobbler', who had gone on two Lions tours. Stuart Evans was on his way to becoming one of the best props in the world when he went to rugby league, Keith Colclough was a few years into an incredibly long and dedicated career with the club and Jeff Herdman was one of the quickest, fittest hookers in Wales.

Richard Moriarty was already established as an international player. Some people were surprised when Dick emerged as Wales captain on the South Pacific tour of 1986, then in the World Cup the following year, but the players who knew him were not. I know he had a reputation as a wild young player, but by the time I got to know him in the mid-1980s he was hugely respected. There was nobody more honest, committed or disciplined in his attitude to the game. He was probably the fittest player at Swansea, which helps explain how he went on playing for so long, and he was intelligent and articulate.

Whether they ever believed any of this at Llanelli, where he was sent off three times, is another matter. Dick and Phil May had a long-running feud, and Dick used to take horrific abuse from the crowd at Stradey. I had an unpleasant time myself at Pontypool when I was keeping David Bishop out of the Wales team, but it was never anything to compare with what Dick had to deal with. The abuse would start as soon as he came on to the field and would continue until the final whistle. It was so bad that his parents refused to go to Stradey.

Dick's younger brother Paul, who was still playing for Swansea in 2000/01 and is the only Welshman to have played in three World Cup semi-finals (one union, two league), was also new to the squad in 1983/4, arriving a few months before me. We were to be capped within two months of each other in 1986, and as two of the youngsters in the squad we naturally enough linked up. Paul is still one of my best friends in rugby – I was the best man at his wedding and we see quite a lot of each other socially. Paul has inherited the family relationship with Stradey; some of the abuse he has taken there over the years has been ludicrous. He is a big, physical guy whose critics have accused him of foul play and violence, but I've always thought of him as a fair player. He is also an exceptional footballer who practises his skills – he will still practise goalkicking as a discipline although it is unlikely the All Whites will ever call on him in a match – and was a very good soccer player at school. A few years ago at Pontypridd he kicked off, ran down the field past two or three tacklers and then chipped ahead to score in the corner. You don't find many back-row forwards who can score a try like that at any age, let alone in their mid-thirties. Paul's dedication and skills, allied to his intelligence, have helped him retain a position as a key member of the All Whites squad long after the age when most of us have retired. His ability to think deeply about and analyse the game, and the knowledge he has built up in a long career embracing both codes of rugby, are likely to make him an outstanding coach.

Gareth Roberts, who played on the flank, was an excellent footballer who was also very physical in his play and would always put his body on the line. Another back-rower was Mike Ruddock, later to become the club coach. Mike was an exceptionally powerful player and a big tackler. There is little doubt that he would have played for Wales but for the back injury from an accident at work that ended his career and sent him into coaching.

This very capable set of forwards was joined a year later by Maurice Colclough, who had scored the winning try for England against the All Blacks in November 1983. Now Maurice had business interests including a couple of restaurants which kept him busy. He would turn up ten minutes before training with his boots and a towel and had pretty much the same approach on match days, often arriving just a quarter of an hour or so before kick-off. As a result, he was never the fittest player, but he was an absolute mountain of a man and a pretty impressive player. I vividly remember him in one match against Richmond. They kicked off, Maurice caught the ball, shouted 'Tally-ho!' and ran straight at the nearest Richmond forward.

The backs oozed talent. Dai Richards and Malcolm Dacey were both world-class players. Dai, who was playing mostly at centre by 1983/4, was a wonderfully smooth, balanced runner and a hugely gifted footballer. He was also full of mischief after he had had a couple of pints, never very far from the nearest fire extinguisher and forever walking up behind people who were reading the *Sporting Post* on Saturday nights in the clubhouse at St Helen's with the intention of setting fire to their papers. Malcolm was a very underrated outside-half with a terrific pair of hands. He was brilliant at getting a back division moving and created as much space for the men outside him as any outside-half I have ever played with. Had there been a Lions tour in the mid-1980s he would certainly have gone on it. He was on the bench, with John Rutherford as first choice, when a Lions team played against the Rest of the World in 1986.

Aled Williams, who was to be a top-class outside-half for years, was just getting going, Mark Wyatt was an international full-back and one of the most accurate kickers in the country, and we had terrific wingers too. Tony Swift lived up to his name and scored dozens of tries for the club, while big Arthur Emyr, who always roared when he got the ball, was the great favourite of the crowd.

I was lucky to play with these men. I was also fortunate to play for a club prepared to give young players their chance. One way in which we hold back the development of young players today is by failing to push them forward early enough. This is largely down to coaches, but you cannot entirely blame them. When you depend on results for your livelihood, as those in the management structure do in the professional game, there is a natural tendency to go for the tried and trusted rather than take the apparent risk of going with a talented but inexperienced youngster. The thinking tends to be that you give them a couple of games this year, perhaps three or four the next, then they'll probably be ready for top-class rugby at 22 or 23. I suspect this may be one reason why the success of Welsh teams at schools and youth level is not carried through to the senior game.

I would not have developed as quickly as I did had Swansea not put their faith in me at an early age. They had done the same with Paul Moriarty and Aled Williams, both of whom were a year or so older than me, and would do so a few years later when Tony Clement, Richard Webster and Dai Young emerged from an extraordinarily good crop of youth players. At other clubs, Neil Jenkins, Scott Gibbs, John Devereux and Jonathan Davies all progressed rapidly into first-class and international rugby.

The attitude ought to be that if a player is good enough, you put him in and keep him in. A player like Gavin Henson, who has made such an impact in 2001 for Swansea, at least two age-group sides and Wales A, needs to be given as many opportunities as possible, and happily there are signs of this happening. I wonder how much further on Craig Morgan, who has always impressed me as a winger, might be had he become a first-team regular earlier in his career. Cardiff, too, are seeing the benefits of placing trust in young talent through the development of Jamie Robinson and Rhys Williams, even if Rhys has struggled a little with his confidence at times. The most successful English clubs have been prepared to put their faith in young players. Leicester have an immensely strong squad, but were still prepared to play eighteen-year-old Ollie Smith at centre in important matches. Newcastle's championship a few years back was won by players they had bought in, but the current team which won the Tetley Bitter Cup is full of players who are 21 or 22 years old.

Of course, it helped that mid-1980s fixture lists included more matches appropriate for trying out young players. My debut against South Wales Police was a good example. It certainly wasn't a soft match – the police had a lot of talent in those days, including Bleddyn Bowen at outside-half. In fact, there was very little that was soft. You were expected to win when you went to Cross Keys on a Wednesday night, but you knew it would be far from easy.

It seems strange from this distance. A current player might well ask how we got motivated when there was nothing in terms of money or league points to play for. But non-competitive does not equal undemanding, and local pride always counted for a great deal. It might only be a few miles from Swansea to Neath or Llanelli, but you never had any doubt that it made a big difference. League points do not need to be at stake to give an edge to local derbies, not when you have more than a hundred years' history as rivals and the knowledge that you and your fans will be hearing all about it from the other team and their fans for the next six months if you don't win. You knew if you were playing well or badly as a team – you didn't need a league table to tell you that – and there was always the element of personal pride in performance: wanting to be the best and to get the better of your opposite number.

Most years, much as it is today, there would be six or seven strong clubs in Wales. There were always strong rivals for me at scrum-half – not just the obvious ones like Terry Holmes and Ray Giles, but someone like Alun Davies at Maesteg, who kicked his team's goals, once dropped a superb goal against us and was a real handful because he was so big and physical. Ironically, he has lost a lot of weight since; had he been carrying less weight when he was playing he might have made even more of his talents. There were formidable opponents in other positions too. Paul Turner, who was playing outside-half at Newbridge, was a superb playmaker, capable of kicking well off either foot in attack and defence. Mark Ring was another – you never knew what he was going to do (you weren't always certain that Mark himself knew). He was always likely to flick the ball over his shoulder or behind his back, to choose the complicated rather than the simple option, but he was dangerous because he had class and unpredictability. I played a part in the knee injury that disrupted his career: he was caught in a double-tackle by me and Mark Davies and his knee went in the collision. Mark never bore any ill will towards us afterwards, recognising that it was just one of those things, but it was unlucky both for him and for Wales.

There were many other players of quality, of course, and that quality went beyond the backs. Lyn Jones in particular springs to mind. Lyn was a terrific loose forward who always gave us trouble when we played Neath and Llanelli. He wasn't very big, but he was horrifyingly quick and, even more importantly, he could think on his feet. He had played scrum-half for Neath and had all the skills. You have to wonder why he did not play more for Wales.

We also had a lot of games against English clubs. Gloucester were our regular opponents at the beginning of the season, the first Saturday in September. That was never an easy start for us, particularly in the years when we had to visit Kingsholm. We played the best and toughest clubs in England, teams like Leicester, Gloucester, Bristol and Bath, but we expected to beat them. We still had a psychological edge in the 1980s when it came to Anglo-Welsh fixtures. We still believed we could beat them with superior football skills. After all, giants of the English game like Maurice Colclough and John Scott were choosing to play in Wales because they thought it provided tougher, more demanding rugby.

We were never complacent, though. A trip to England was always important to us, although not always straightforward, as I found on a trip to Blackheath in November 1986 that provided one of the more embarrassing moments of my Swansea career. I travelled up in my car along with two of our front-rowers, Carl Yates and Hugh Gilson. We were fine until we reached the suburbs of London, where we lost our way. We kept on asking the way and eventually wound up in Blackheath – unfortunately not the one in south-east London, but a village near Guildford. No wonder people there looked surprised when we asked the way to the rugby ground! This was before the days of mobile phones, so we had a desperate job getting through to Jeff Herdman, the coach, to tell him what had happened. There was no way we could make it to the right Blackheath in time for kick-off, so Clive Williams, who had recently retired, had to play and Jeff was on the bench. The following week someone placed an advert in the Swansea programme: 'Wanted urgently – road map and/or *Visitors' Guide to London*, will exchange for *Interesting Journeys Around Guildford* (rather worn). Please reply to: R. Jones, Club House, Swansea RFC'. Since it was the last time the Whites played Blackheath, I never got another chance to prove I could find the place.

We won that game 16–6, our confidence in being able to beat English clubs generally justified. I don't remember many defeats against English opposition, although there were certainly some extremely tough games. The regular contact reinforced that confidence, which we carried through into internationals. I have no doubt it was one of the reasons why Wales had such a good record against England. It also provided variety in the season and stopped us getting either parochial or bored with playing only a limited number of opponents.

Our fixture list from the early and mid-1980s may look strange to modern eyes, but ironically we have spent the last few years trying to get back to something like it: tough domestic opposition plus the variety provided by an Anglo-Welsh element. I think we lost out badly after 1987 when the Courage League was formed in England. Anglo-Welsh fixtures continued for several years, but were a much lower priority for clubs which also had league games to play. Variety and depth slowly disappeared from our fixture lists. In the absence of regular contact with English clubs, Wales has developed something of an inferiority complex which I believe has contributed to some heavy defeats by England in the last ten years of internationals.

We had a succession of coaches at Swansea in the 1980s. Ian Hall was in charge when I arrived, a South Wales policeman and former international centre who was very aggressive and a strong motivator. Stan Addicott from Swansea University, who had been coach before Ian, returned for a season when Ian left, and we also had spells with Jeff Herdman, Alun Donovan, Mike Heath, Trevor James and Alan Lewis before Mike Ruddock took over in 1991. Inevitably, there were differences in personality and coaching style, but what they all had in common was that they had come from within the club – all of them apart from Stan had played for it – and had a strong sense of the way Swansea teams were expected to play.

That style had a lot to do with playing at St Helen's. It was always a superb playing surface, probably the best in Wales, ideal except in the worst weather for playing an open, attacking style of rugby. And of course we had the backs and the footballing forwards capable of playing that way. But there was perhaps a downside to this. Because we were so accustomed to St Helen's, we always seemed to be a little vulnerable in difficult conditions away from home. We tended to be inconsistent under those circumstances and had a history of lapses in the cup, losing to teams like Glamorgan Wanderers. When you consider how often we ranked among the strongest teams in Wales, it was a hopeless underachievement not to win the cup for the second time until 1995. By that time Llanelli had won it nine times.

Those cup failures were frustrating, the succession of coaches was a touch inconvenient, but there was little else wrong with the club. The rugby was always hugely enjoyable. We wanted to do well and were given the freedom to play our rugby in a relaxed fashion. Progress towards leagues and professionalism was inevitable, but I would not have been unhappy had my whole career been played under the structures and conditions we enjoyed in Welsh club rugby in the 1980s.

It was a very different world, psychologically and financially. The emphasis was on enjoyment; you played out of choice rather than obligation. One of the things that always used to amuse me when we played against England or English clubs, or played with English players in invitation teams like the Barbarians, was that they believed Welsh players were being paid a lot of money. One of the most famous stories was that Jonathan Davies was being paid the proceeds from the car park at Stradey. This would have been a tidy amount, but the story was complete and utter nonsense. There was a small amount of money in Welsh rugby, but it certainly was not anything you could hope to live on.

When I started at Swansea at the back end of 1983, we were paid £5 per game, which went straight into the players' kitty for our tour to Barbados, plus travelling expenses which worked out for me at about £40 per month. By 1986/7 we were getting about £20 for a win; then in 1990, when the league came in, we were paid £20 for a loss and £40 for a win. If we won two matches in a row that went up to £50, then £70 and £90 for further consecutive wins, although the escalator stopped there. Expenses were calculated at around 20p per mile. Those rates stayed pretty much unchanged until I left the club in 1996. This was, of course, in breach of the regulations on amateurism, but they were certainly not the sort of sums that could be considered a living wage, particularly as you did not get paid if you did not play. Everybody was doing it – and by everybody I don't just mean all the Welsh clubs. English clubs were doing the same, so were South African provinces. And it was all completely above board with the Inland Revenue.

The big change during the pre-professional years at Swansea was the introduction of the league system in 1990. It was inevitable, once England had its leagues, that we would go the same way. The fixtures against their clubs which had been such an important part of our season had lost a great deal of their meaning and were fading away. We could also see that England, where the club game was not traditionally as strong as it had been in Wales, was benefiting from the introduction of leagues and the national team was looking a great deal stronger. Being beaten 34–6 at Twickenham in February 1990, after the introduction of leagues had been agreed but before they had started, was a painful reminder we would rather have done without.

The league looked like the way forward in Wales too, and initially it was successful, helping raise interest in club rugby. There was undoubtedly a change in attitudes within clubs. There was suddenly greater emphasis on results and less on enjoyment or the quality of rugby played. Coaches became more important and interventionist, more and more obsessed with video analysis and set moves. But I felt that the momentum from the novelty of it was lost after a couple of seasons and we got rather bored with playing the same small group of opponents. I am still to be convinced that the introduction of leagues has been beneficial in Wales. There is clearly no going back to the days when most matches were amateur, but I feel we have not benefited nearly as much from the change as other countries, particularly England.

Having said that, some of the best moments of my club career came in the period between 1990 and 1995. One reason for this was the coaching of Mike Ruddock, who took over in 1991. He came back to us after spending some time in Ireland coaching Bective Rangers – a sensible move on his part to broaden his experience and knowledge at the same time as learning the job of coaching without the pressures that go with the job in Wales. The atmosphere in Ireland was much more relaxed, and Mike came back to us an extremely accomplished trainer who thought very deeply about the game. One of the consistent notes in press reports on the Whites in the 1980s was the 'need for greater consistency and more steel up front'. Mike succeeded in instilling these qualities. He ensured that we were not found wanting at the set pieces or in terms of the hard graft which was his hallmark as a player, and concentrated at the same time on the need for our forwards to be good with the ball in their hands.

Although Mike was determined that we should be a disciplined side, he was not the sort of coach who tells you what to do. He gave senior players responsibility and encouraged us to be ourselves. He also saw his coaching responsibilities as going beyond rugby into areas of off-the-field man-management. Mike wanted us all to get on as a group, and worked very hard at creating a family atmosphere at the club. At least once a month there was an event at the clubhouse – a disco or some such entertainment – to which players, wives and girlfriends were invited. If we went out for a couple of drinks, everyone would go, all of which helped create a spirit that contributed to our success.

Mike also had some good players to work with, not least in his own former position of back row. Richard Webster was desperately unlucky after a brilliant start to his international career at the 1987 World Cup. Given the succession of injuries and operations he suffered, the wonder was that

Webby came back to play senior rugby at all. He was an interesting character to have around because he was astonishingly competitive and refused to be beaten at anything. If a team-mate could do something or he heard another back row could do it, he would want to do it better. Running up mountains, knocking down elephants – whatever it was, Webby had to prove that he could do it better. Alan Reynolds, another very tough flanker, was exactly the same, so he and Webby were endlessly competing with each other at just about any activity you can think of.

This 'rivalry' reached a peak on tour one year when they were playing darts in a bar in Florida. After a while they started to throw the darts at each other, and the competition soon became to see which of them could get a dart to stick in the other. They agreed that the loser would have to try to stop with his hand a huge fan whose blades were revolving at great speed. Alan lost and – I won't say to our amazement, because by then nothing he and Webby got up to surprised us – tried to stick his hand in the fan. How on earth he came away without losing it, I'll never know.

Alan's competitiveness was put to more positive use on the field. He was the type who would have played the same way against Trebanos down the park and Cardiff at the Arms Park. He was incapable of giving less than one hundred per cent. He was not the biggest flanker in Wales, but he made up for that with effort, commitment and a willingness to put his body on the line whenever it mattered. He won a couple of caps and probably deserved more.

By this time, Stuart Davies was well established at number eight. Stuart and I had known each other since under-13 level – at which age he already had a reputation as a good player, and Mumbles were a useful team because of him – and became team-mates for Wales Schools at the age of fifteen. We grew up together in rugby terms and built up an extremely good understanding of each other's strengths and weaknesses. We did not agree on everything, however. Stuart was very definite about the fact that scoring pushover tries was the number eight's job, and he proved his point by scoring quite a few. Occasionally I thought it was my job, but since I would normally have had to run around Stuart's backside – a considerable journey which required a lot of stamina – I did not get my own way very often. He was another highly intelligent, thinking footballer, a graduate of the South Glamorgan Institute with a great ability to put people into space. He was vital to Swansea; we were never really quite the same force when he was not there. Mentally we were not quite as confident or as sure in our judgement of plays when Stuart was absent.

The regular outside-half was Aled Williams. He is a little older than me, but also broke in early and we played together as half-backs against the Australian tourists in 1984. The papers made something of Swansea putting out teenage half-backs, remembering Haydn Tanner and Willie Davies, both of whom were still at school, playing together when the All Blacks were beaten in 1935, but the game was mainly memorable for the fact that the floodlights failed. It was a bit of a blessing in disguise as Australia were playing very well, and we were not.

Aled went to Bridgend for a while in the mid-1980s, but he returned to become an immense asset to the Whites. He was a classic old-style outside-half, a superb distributor and runner who was very quick off the mark. He was a good goalkicker and line-kicker too, but never totally consistent. Had his kicking been better he might have added another twenty caps to his tally; he was certainly a better player than his two caps would suggest. He formed an excellent partnership with Scott Gibbs, who was very good at taking advantage of Aled's ability to create gaps. Scott had come to Swansea from Neath after Webby, Tony Clement and I worked hard on him during the 1991 tour of Australia – so at least some good came out of that tour, although you would not expect anyone from Neath to agree.

Tony Clement was another player who became a very good friend. It might seem odd to speak of someone who won 37 caps and went on two Lions tours as an underachiever, but I think he was. Tony was one of the most gifted players I ever played with or against, one of those people who seemed to be able to do anything he wanted on a rugby field. In some ways that was his problem: he was an international-class player almost anywhere in the back division except scrum-half, and as a result he was always being moved around for the convenience of the team. This made it difficult for him to claim any position as definitely his own.

During the first half of the 1990s, as I said, Swansea gave me moments to match anything in my career. There is something special about your first cap and your fiftieth, and being selected for and playing in a test match for the Lions, but winning championships in 1992 and 1994, beating Australia at St Helen's in 1992 and the cup win in 1995 were definitely occasions to match them.

The night we beat Australia, 4 October 1992, was an outstanding one. They had won the World Cup only the year before. In my memories of the matches I've played against them, one of the best – the third-place World Cup match in June 1987 when we beat them 22–21 – had been crowded out by two nightmares from 1991: the disastrous tour there and the 38–3 beating they inflicted on us at the National Stadium in October during the World Cup. They sent down a pretty good side considering it was a midweek match, including Phil Kearns, John Eales, Jason Little and Tim Horan. The conditions weren't great for rugby, very wet and blustery; we had to defend pretty determinedly when the wind was behind them, then keep them pinned into their own half when we had the advantage. We outplayed them to win 21–6. Nobody could believe it, and I was particularly delighted for Keith Colclough. Cloughie was a real club stalwart and technically one of the best props I ever played with. He completely demolished his opposite number. He played for the Whites for years – he is still involved in the Swansea set-up now – and was unlucky not to receive any outside recognition other than selection for the Barbarians. Only the weekend before I had been in a French Barbarians team (it was Serge Blanco's last match) that had beaten the Springboks. I don't think many players have been in teams that have beaten South Africa and Australia in the space of four days.

Beating Pontypridd in the 1995 Cup Final was special as well. I was starting to think that I was never going to get a cup winner's medal – I was coming up to thirty and beginning to wonder if time was running out. I had played in two losing finals, to Cardiff in 1987 and Llanelli in 1992, and my brother Rhodri had been a runner-up as well, for Neath against Llanelli in 1993. When we won the championship in 1992 it was, believe it or not, the first winner's medal I had received since sevens competitions at school. The cup medal completed the set.

It also marked a crucial point in my career. My international career was to finish only weeks after that win over Pontypridd, in June when we were knocked out of the World Cup by Ireland in Johannesburg. The game was about to go professional, the deal between the three big southern hemisphere unions and Rupert Murdoch was concluded during the World Cup and the International Rugby Board's acceptance of the inevitable came at the end of August. The cup win came at the end of my twelfth season at Swansea. I expected to spend the rest of my career with them. Had you told me that in a year's time I would be at another club, I would have laughed at the thought.

# **6** Turning Pro

'I did not want to leave Swansea, but I went on an issue of principle. The club had agreed a playing contract with me but had never offered me the chance to sign it. Maybe they thought the contract to work with Dan Minster incorporated the playing contract, but if they did they didn't say so, and I wouldn't have accepted on those terms anyway. I would have been happy to stay for less than the packages offered by Harlequins and Bristol, but they were not prepared to offer me a £12,000 contract that was already agreed.'

N OBODY WAS PREPARED for the shift to professionalism or recognised its full implications. We have learned them the hard way in the six or so years since, a period of instability and panic which has still really to end. The problems were most visible at the top end of the game where clubs like Llanelli found themselves having to pay ridiculous amounts of money in order to compete with the likes of Cardiff, but without the financial backing clubs like Cardiff, Newcastle and Richmond enjoyed. Llanelli got into serious financial trouble, but it is not clear that they were wrong to do so. Llanelli have always been one of our great clubs, and they have retained that status. They feared that if they did not try to compete, they would be knocked aside in the professional era. By comparison, Newport, who kept their house in order in the early days, found they could not compete until they found a wealthy backer.

There were also problems much further down the scale. Within six to twelve months of the announcement by the IRB you started to hear of clubs playing quite a low level of rugby yet paying £15, £50 or even in some cases £100 per game to players. It was ludicrous. In the context of the level of rugby they were playing and the income of the clubs, there was no way they were worth £100, or even £15. Trebanos, who were not prepared to pay, lost good players to those who would.

Clubs were thrown into an entirely new world for which they were totally unprepared. Previously, players had been volunteers, turning out because they wanted to, the registration form the only formal relationship with the club. To the clubs, we were members. That relationship changed out of all recognition. Clubs became employers; players ceased to be members and became employees, contracts binding both sides. It was hardly surprising that both clubs and players took a while to adjust to these new obligations.

Swansea did not adjust. By the end of my thirteenth season there a series of events had led to my leaving the club with which I, and they, thought I would play my whole career. Up to that point, joining another club had never even entered my mind. I had gone to South Africa to play for Western Province in the summer of 1994 and following the World Cup in 1995, but always on the clear understanding that I would be returning to St Helen's as soon as their season was over.

I had always been happy at Swansea. There were occasional irritations, of course. I could not help noticing, for instance, the way Llanelli commemorated the landmarks in Ieuan Evans' career. When Ieuan won his fiftieth cap and received his MBE, the club recognised and celebrated those achievements. When I won my fiftieth, just ahead of Ieuan, I received letters and telegrams from people and clubs all over the world of rugby, but nothing from my own club. There was no mention of it in the programme or at the club dinner, and it was the same with my MBE. I was only the third Welshman to win fifty caps, following Gareth Edwards and J.P.R. Williams. I was told that Baden Evans, the rugby manager, had said, 'We're waiting for Rob to become the most capped player' – which of course never happened.

At the end of the 1993/4 season we beat Aberavon to win our second championship in three seasons. I was due to play in South Africa, but had told the club I would wait until the championship was settled. Earlier in the week, Clem Thomas, whose views rightly carried immense weight at Swansea, had written in his column in the *Evening Post* that 'Robert Jones is going to South Africa to play for Western Province, where I hope he will be more appreciated than he has been in his

home club of Swansea'. After the game, club chairman Mike
James called all the pressmen together in the clubhouse and
announced that I was going to be awarded a club loyalty cap,
reviving a tradition which had died out in the 1920s. Of
course I was delighted, although I did point out that Richard
Moriarty and Keith Colclough, both of whom were playing
that day, had been with the club longer than I had. I was told,
'Don't worry, we'll be doing something for them later in the
year.' Roger Blyth, who was on the committee, told me
afterwards how chastened everyone had felt after reading
Thomas's article, that they wanted to show how much I
meant to them.

Byron Mugford, the club secretary, had a cap in a cello-
phane bag. He explained that it wasn't the real cap, which
would be specially made and presented to me on my return
from South Africa. Unfortunately, there was no sign of it
when I did get back. Every so often I asked about it; it was
on order and would be arriving shortly. I probably asked
about a dozen times in all. Eventually it became embarrassing. The cap still had not been presented when I left in 1996,
and to this day in 2001 I have not received it, although it was
reported at the time in the press and the story appears in the
club's official history. Nor was anything ever done for Dick
and Keith, both of whom are still at the club – Dick as team
manager, Keith helping with coaching – after more than
twenty years.

All of this was irritating and disappointing, particularly
because I was so delighted by the award at the time. But in
comparison to the enjoyment I got out of playing for the club
over the years, it did not matter very much. Then came the
announcement in 1995 that professionalism was to be allowed, and a flow of newspaper stories and rumours went around
clubs about who was going where and for how much.

Early in 1996, I was approached by Harlequins. I went up
there with Phil Davies, who had also been approached. We
met Dick Best, whom I had got to know and like on the 1993
Lions tour, and Phil and I were offered contracts for more

money than I had ever seen. I was on £18,000 at the time in my job with CE Heath, the insurance brokers run by Ian Brice and Brynmor Williams; Quins were offering £35,000 basic plus £1,500 per match, a £500 win bonus and rental and car allowances – and I could still work part-time with CE Heath at their London office if I wanted to.

I immediately made Mike Ruddock and other people at Swansea aware of the approach. The offer from Harlequins was extremely tempting; if the game was going professional, I had to think about my future and I had a young family to consider. A month or so later I was looking at property in London and my solicitor had gone through the contract with Harlequins, but nothing much was happening at Swansea, so I went down to the club and reminded them, 'I'm about to sign for Harlequins.' Their reaction was, 'Hang about, you've been here all your life, you can't be serious?' To which I replied, 'I am being serious. I've let you know what is going on and kept you informed all the way.'

A meeting was called with the officials of the club, and they came up with a package where for three days a week I would do commercial work for the club alongside Dan Minster, who was chief executive at the time. That was going to pay me £20,000 and reduce my hours with CE Heath to two days a week. In addition, I had introduced Terry Ryan, the managing director of Cabletel – now ntl – to the club and I negotiated a £10,000 package with them to do public relations work. It was also agreed that once all this had been sorted out I would be given in addition a £12,000 part-time rugby contract to play for the club. I was more than happy with this. The total package was much more than I had ever seen before and I had not wanted to leave home anyway.

I turned Quins down and waited patiently to sign my player's contract with Swansea. Existing and new players were signing part-time contracts worth £10,000, £12,000 or £15,000, but nothing happened on my contract. A couple of months later I found myself on the same table as Baden Evans at a dinner in the Brangwyn Hall and said to him,

'Bade, you've done everybody else's contract – when are you going to do mine?' He replied, 'Rob, are you being serious? So far as we're concerned everything is settled.' So we had another meeting the next day. I pointed out to him that the other negotiated contracts had nothing to do with the rugby side of things. I had no contract as a player with the club, even though I had sat down with Mike James and agreed a £12,000 deal. Baden said, 'I know nothing about this. It isn't in the budget.'

Several more weeks went by and I heard nothing from the club. But in the meantime I did discover that Rhodri, my younger brother who had been the other scrum-half at the club since I had persuaded him to move from Neath, had been told by Kevin Hopkins, our backs coach, that he was going to be the number one scrum-half for the coming season. Nobody had thought to tell me, and Rhod had naturally felt uncomfortable about it because he didn't want to tell me himself. The extraordinary thing was that Kevin and I were extremely good friends. We had just been on holiday together for a fortnight in Majorca with our wives and children. I had been going out running with Kev and saying things like, 'I'm really going for it this summer, we're going to have a really great season.' I of course wanted Rhodri to progress, and when he came back to Swansea Mike Ruddock said to us, 'Whoever is playing best will be number one.' I was quite happy with that. What upset me was that I had no inkling of the changes afoot. It had all been done behind my back.

It was at this point, sometime in May, that I received a call from Dave Tyler at Bristol. He told me that they had lost Kyran Bracken to Saracens and wanted somebody of international quality to replace him. He asked if I would join them for £50,000 and a car. I explained that I had agreed to stay with Swansea, but that if I heard of another scrum-half who was on the market, I would let him know. When I put the phone down my wife Meg asked me what it was about. I explained the offer and told her what I had said. She said,

'There's something not quite right here,' which made me think about the call and what I was potentially turning down. Once I'd realised she was right, I rang Dave Tyler back and said that I was interested after all and wanted to sign.

I went down to the Swansea club and told Mike Ruddock I was signing for Bristol. He said, 'I understand why you are doing it. You've been taken for granted here.' Then I sat down and wrote letters to the main club officials explaining why I was leaving, and drove around Swansea delivering them by hand before I went off to play in Philippe Sella's testimonial match in Agen. When I got to France, Mike phoned me. 'Rob,' he said, 'have you definitely signed for Bristol? Rhodri has injured his shoulder playing in the Student World Cup and we haven't got a scrum-half.' I had to tell him that I had signed.

I did not want to leave Swansea, but I went on an issue of principle. The club had agreed a playing contract with me but had never offered me the chance to sign it. Maybe they thought the contract to work with Dan Minster incorporated the playing contract, but if they did they didn't say so, and I wouldn't have accepted on those terms anyway. I would have been happy to stay for less than the packages offered by Harlequins and Bristol, but they were not prepared to offer me a £12,000 contract that was already agreed. Mike Ruddock was right. I felt taken for granted, that the club's attitude was 'Don't worry about Rob. He's a one-club man, part of the furniture. We know he'll never leave.' Ironically, after telling me there was nothing in the budget to cover my £12,000 they ended up having to find more money. They were so worried that they might lose other senior players that they offered two of them £25,000 – considerably more than they had been told they were going to get.

I had been offered a testimonial year at Swansea as a reward for past services. I was sufficiently piqued by this stage to give up on the testimonial, but my committee said they had a few events organised and would like to carry on, and Bristol said they'd put a match on. There was also a testimonial dinner in the Brangwyn Hall in Swansea, to which three or four hundred people came. Llanelli and Dunvant rugby clubs were among those who took tables. Swansea rugby club pulled out the morning before the dinner.

I thought I was joining a strong club in Bristol. I had played against them often enough in my earlier days at Swansea and was aware of their history, tradition and status as one of England's top clubs. Alan Davies, for whom I'd had a great deal of respect when he was Wales coach, was in charge of the playing side of things. The club was building a new stand at the ground, which had a lovely playing surface almost up to St Helen's standards. And I was joining some players of note. Paul Hull, who was unlucky not to play far more often for England, was at full-back. The outside-half was Paul Burke, and there was another high-quality Irish international, David Corkery, playing in the back row. Martin Corry, an international-quality player in the back or second row, was the captain, and the front row included Alan Sharp, who propped for Scotland, and Mark Regan, who was to go on the 1997 Lions tour as second choice to Keith Wood at hooker.

But things didn't work out. The English game was a couple of steps ahead of the Welsh game by 1995. There was no doubt it was more professional and there was far greater competitive depth. It was not that there were tougher or more intense matches than Swansea versus Llanelli or Cardiff, but there were certainly more difficult games, and none you could take for granted. Clubs like Newcastle and Leicester had put together awesomely strong squads, and in the end Bristol simply did not have the resources to compete. We started the 1996/7 season reasonably well, winning three of our first five matches, but after that it was an uphill battle and we had to beat Bedford in the play-offs just to stay in the First Division.

In my second season, I was made captain – Martin Corry had gone to Leicester – and it was another desperate struggle for the club. Bath had poached Mark Regan and they'd asked me as well, but I was under contract to Bristol for another season. Sadly, Bristol's financial position was a major concern throughout 1997/8. Even Alan was not always too sure what was going on, and he left midway through the season, which was a real blow. The players tried to put it all to the backs of their minds and concentrate on playing, but with so much turmoil and uncertainty it was very hard. We won only two games all season, were relegated after we lost both legs of the play-off to London Scottish and also went out of the cup to Worcester. As captain, I had to listen to the players' feelings and anxieties about their futures and take them to board members. I remember that July going to lunch with Arthur Holmes, club president and the main backer, and coming out feeling reassured about the club's future.

Not long after that lunch the players were called to a meeting with the management where they were told the club was being put into receivership. We felt let down, to put it mildly. I was about to sign a new two-year contract. Players like Kevin Maggs were furious and called the management bloody liars. All this happened just before Meg, Emily and I went on holiday to Ibiza, so I spent almost as much time on the phone to other players as I did relaxing with my family.

When I got back to England there were two consortia bidding for the club: one was led by the people who owned Bristol City FC and John Burke, chief executive of the Bristol and West Building Society, who were our main sponsors. I had a very good relationship with John and felt he and his group were the right people to take over. Had they done so I would happily have signed again with Bristol and taken on the challenge of getting them back into the Premiership. I would have been quite content to spend the rest of my career with them, although it was always at the back of my mind that I would like to finish back at Swansea. Then, out of the blue, it was awarded to a second group led by businessman and former Bristol player Nick de Scoscia, and they came in and took control. Unlike John's consortium, they had not talked to the players and were keeping their cards very close to their chests, so it was not clear what we could expect.

At around this time, during the close season, Peter Thomas contacted me and asked me to join Cardiff. I was worried about the situation at Bristol: I was not being paid and was not happy about being taken over by people we knew nothing about. When Bob Dwyer came in I was offered a new contract, but by that time I had decided I would be happier to move to Cardiff. I knew and liked Peter Thomas and had a great deal of respect for the chief executive, Gareth Davies. It was also thirty miles closer to home, giving me more time to develop my business interests outside the game.

Another reason for going to Cardiff was that I had never totally given up hope of playing for my country again. I knew it was an extremely long shot – I was coming up to 33 when the 1998/9 season started and had not been in a Wales squad for three years – but there is a lot to be said for setting yourself ambitious targets as a way of motivating yourself. Joining the same club as Robert Howley, firmly established at scrum-half for Wales, and competing with him for the club number nine shirt was as good a way as any of trying to be noticed again.

I enjoyed playing at Cardiff and had some excellent team-mates there, but it still felt strange putting on their shirt – never stranger than the day when we played Swansea at St Helen's. It was hard putting on the blue and black shirt in the wrong dressing room, knowing that my brother and a lot of my best friends in rugby were in the other room, that my mates were in the stand or on the terraces supporting the other team. Swansea played well, and we were hammered. I remember the hardest moments coming at half-time. Terry Holmes, our coach, came into the changing room, and to try to get us motivated he started slagging off the Swansea players – my brother among them – saying they were not as good as us and we should not be losing to them. I remember thinking, 'I'm a professional, I have an obligation to play as well as I can. But I don't like what I'm hearing.'

However, you cannot dispute the fact that Cardiff are one of the great clubs in world rugby, with a history and tradition to match anybody's. In a time when many Welsh clubs lack the resources enjoyed by their English rivals, Cardiff have been able to compete. There is always a lot of talent at the club, and there is little doubt that they should have won the European Cup by now. Instead, they have not even been the most successful club in Wales. Swansea have won four championships to their two, and Llanelli have been the dominant force in the cup. It is hard to explain why. One possible explanation is that they lack players of the kind they used to have, people like Bob Lakin and Tim Crothers who came up through the club and were its life and soul. Cardiff have always had players from other parts of Wales – it is that sort of place, that kind of club – mixed with people who have grown up in Cardiff and come through the 'Rags', who see it as their only possible club. That feeling always gives a little bit extra to your play, and maybe Cardiff have lacked it in recent years.

So going back to my club, Swansea, for my last season made a lot of sense, although it probably would not have happened when it did had I not been involved, in June 1999, in a nasty car crash with Meg, Rhodri and his fiancée Helen. I was knocked out and suffered injuries to my sternum, while Rhod's arm was broken. A policeman who was in the other car was killed. It was a horrible experience, and it took a while for me to get my motivation back. Certainly the thought of travelling to Cardiff every day to train was impossible. They agreed to release me, so I was able to go back to Swansea, where I could develop other opportunities and also fill in at scrum-half while Rhod was recovering from his longer-term injuries.

I sat straight down with Swansea and we agreed a part-time deal giving me £7,000 plus £200 per win. I can't say I was happy with this as I doubt any other player, apart perhaps from the odd apprentice, was on so little money. My contract at Cardiff had been worth £45,000 and the best-paid players at Swansea were on anything between £70,000 and £120,000, so I had hoped for a little more, to say the least. But my desire to return to Swansea and finish my career where I had started far outweighed any financial considerations.

I had expected to go to training perhaps a couple of times a week and devote most of my energies to other activities I was pursuing. Instead, for the first few months I found that I was virtually full-time, hardly missing a training session. I played most of the matches until the end of November, won the odd Man of the Match award, and was enjoying it enormously. There were some memorable moments too, like the match against Llanelli at St Helen's where Arwel Thomas dropped two late goals to give us the points. The idea always was that I would step aside when Rhod returned, but I expected that I would still play the odd match after that. It seemed to me that it would make sense to rest Rhod occasionally. Coming back from an injury as serious as the one he had suffered takes time, and I expected him to be eased in. Instead, John Plumtree, the Swansea coach, played Rhodri in almost every match. I was not even on the bench.

After November I featured in just one match – the last ten minutes of the game against Edinburgh at St Helen's the following April. They gave me Man of the Match as a token gesture, but I must admit I had hoped to finish on a slightly higher note. Swansea did get to the 2000 Cup Final, where we were beaten by Llanelli (some things in Welsh rugby just don't seem to change!), and I travelled with the boys on the team bus, but in no other way was I involved. Quite what I did wrong at the back end of 1999, when I thought things had been going reasonably well, I do not know. I must admit I had also hoped that a few words might be said about my retirement at the annual dinner, but there was nothing. The end was rather anticlimactic, which was a shame after fourteen seasons with the club.

I am not the only player to have ended his career at Swansea rather disappointed in recent years. Stuart Davies, too, was hurt when he was forced to retire with an injury he received playing for Wales. A week or so later he received a formal letter from the club cancelling his contract and asking for the return of his car. I doubt Swansea were doing anything legally wrong, but Stuart had been at the club since he was at school. He had given them tremendous service, playing first-team rugby there for twelve years – most of them as an amateur – and was captain for two seasons, in one of which we won a league championship. Being thrown out with a few days' notice seemed abrupt and ungrateful. Fortunately, Stuart had never given up his job in environmental health with Swansea Council, so he was not thrown onto the dole queue, but he still felt pretty disillusioned by the experience.

It was hard not to be struck by the contrast when the South African Gary Teichmann left Newport at the end of the 2000/01 season. The club arranged a Gary Teichmann day at the end of the season to celebrate his contribution towards reviving Newport over two seasons. Now I'm not saying I begrudge Gary any of that. He did a superb job for Newport, not just as a player but as a leader and an example to everyone at the club. They could not have achieved nearly as much as they did in a short time without him. But he had been at Newport for two years. When you join a club from school and play for it for well over a decade, you might hope for at least a tap on the back.

Yet I still love Swansea, and I always will. The loyalties generated by clubs are vitally important to Welsh rugby; they give the game its meaning. To take one example, there is no doubt that Llanelli are one of the great names not just in Welsh but in world rugby. They have produced an endless stream of great players and some superb teams, as we at Swansea have often found to our cost, particularly in cup ties. Yet I cannot imagine for one moment playing for them. The feelings between Swansea and Llanelli and their supporters are so strong that it would feel like a betrayal. Cardiff felt strange enough, but Llanelli would have been impossible. Professionalism inevitably changes these things, but it still seems strange to me to see Neil Jenkins, who is as rooted in his background as I am in Trebanos, playing for anybody other than Pontypridd. Being Neil, he does a terrific job, but I would guess that it still feels a bit odd to him.

Clubs are the basis of our game. Every so often you get calls for our game to be reorganised on a regional basis, with provinces devised to raise the standard of our best players. It simply would not work. It works for New Zealand, Ireland and South Africa where they have a history of provincial rugby so those identities mean something. We don't have that. You can't invent identities. You certainly can't make people care about them. So we have to build on our clubs, their history and their traditions. It may not be ideal, but that is the way it is.

Graham Henry's proposal for 'superclubs' to play in Europe made no sense. It envisaged Neath linking up with Swansea, Bridgend with Cardiff. I cannot see the supporters of either Neath or Bridgend, who would have been junior partners in these set-ups, being prepared to back the new team. They would either have gone back to supporting junior clubs in their district – which you might argue would be no bad thing – or been lost to rugby altogether. Furthermore, under the terms of the proposal Neath and Bridgend, who have consistently produced quality players – hanging on to them has been their problem – would have lost their identities while Newport, who have fewer Wales-qualified players than any other leading club, would have been freestanding. Henry has also said that he wants to see national squad players getting regular rugby rather than sitting on the bench, yet his idea would have created clubs with squads of forty or more players.

The previous superclub concept, with the Welsh Rugby Union concentrating its support on four or possibly five clubs, was just as flawed. It would have made our domestic competitions less, not more, competitive with the clubs outside the elite group falling further and further behind. We already have a dominant group of four or five clubs to whom the best players naturally gravitate. It would be daft and counterproductive to institutionalise that. It would be saying to clubs like Neath, who were league champions only five years ago, that they could never aspire to that status again. We should also retain promotion and relegation – only one team between the top two divisions, but it must be kept. The alternative is to tell Aberavon and Pontypool, both formerly great clubs, that they are doomed to permanent second-class status. There may be a quicker and more efficient way of turning people away from rugby, but I can't think of one. Indeed, promotion and relegation should run all the way down the leagues. Trebanos won't ever play at the top level, but there is no reason why they should not aspire to rise a division or two on their merits. If we deny hope and ambition, we start undermining the identities on which Welsh rugby has always been based.

At the same time we should be encouraging clubs outside the top league to go back to amateurism. I agree with David Pickering, who has said that it is ludicrous for there to be 600 professional rugby players in Wales. It is far too many, and we simply cannot afford it. Of course we want our players to aspire to be professionals, but this ambition should only be achieved if they are good enough. Ideally, only the top division should be professional. I accept that you cannot ban payments further down – contracts have been signed and agreements made – but they should be discouraged. The Welsh Rugby Union's plan to make grants to lower-division clubs only for specific projects, and only to pay when invoices are presented showing that work has been done, is a step in the right direction. The second highest division would obviously have to be a sort of transition zone, with the more ambitious and better resourced clubs employing some professionals and a system of cushioning payments so clubs that are relegated do not go broke and those that are promoted are not hopelessly uncompetitive. But nobody outside the top two divisions should be getting paid.

The question of how you structure the leagues and the season is a tricky one, but in my opinion we have been getting it wrong so far. There have been almost non-stop changes, many of them nonsensical and instituted at extremely short notice. The creation of the Celtic League – Irish teams alongside teams in the existing Welsh-Scottish League – is a classic example. I had always assumed that the idea was simply to extend the Welsh-Scottish League, bringing in the Irish provinces to make it more competitive. Everybody I spoke to had made the same assumption. So I could not believe it when it was announced that it would be an additional competition, running alongside the Welsh-Scottish League. There are good reasons why simply extending the Welsh-Scottish League was impossible – the Irish clubs were totally opposed to their provincial teams becoming full-time professional outfits; they and their league would have been downgraded – but given those problems, you have to wonder why the Celtic League is being created at all. There seems little point in having two competitions which overlap so much.

I do, however, think a cross-border dimension to our season is essential. So do the clubs and players of every other country in the Six Nations. But we have already seen the difficulties involved in trying to extend the current Welsh-Scottish League to include the Irish provinces. We would also like to see the return of regular Anglo-Welsh fixtures, but we have now been trying for some time with little success. However desirable the outcome may be, we can't wait for ever.

My feeling is that we need to think past Celtic, Anglo-Welsh or British league proposals towards expanded European competitions. That, of course, introduces its own complications. When you consider how difficult we managed to make life by ourselves, it is not hard to see that solutions involving several unions could prove very elusive. Each union has its own structures, sponsorships and television agreements, all expiring at different times, and those agreements must be honoured. But sponsorship and television deals rarely last more than three or four years before they are up for renewal. The unions need to sit down and fix on a date – no matter if it's three or four years away – when they can have a blank sheet on which to sort out a joint future. Any set of structures agreed should be put in place for at least five years, because we desperately need some stability. Clubs must start one season knowing what they are playing for in terms of the next.

As part of this deal, leading players should not be expected to play more than about thirty matches a season (still more than an Australian plays). They should also be guaranteed three months with no matches in the summer. The top players are playing too much at the moment, and this is detrimental to their health and to the quality of entertainment they can offer. The clubs might worry that this leaves them with fewer fixtures, and thus less income, but I don't think that would happen. If your best players are fitter and fresher, the standard of play and entertainment should rise, enthusing the fans.

Expanding the European Cup, for instance, would build on a successful existing structure rather than trying to tear up the current season and start again. We know that European rugby excites fans, players and even members of the media. It produces quality rugby. We have had our share of disappointments in Wales, particularly in 2000/01 when our teams started so well but fell away badly in the second phase of the competition. If the group stages had been completed instead of being halted for three months after we had started so well in October, I believe we would have had two or three teams topping the groups and getting home draws that would have given them an excellent chance of getting through to the semi-finals. We do need to get away from the stop-start structure of the competition – and I am not just saying that because it was bad for the Welsh clubs this season. You will hear exactly the same argument from someone like François Pienaar at Saracens.

My preference would be to extend the pool stage so that there are six teams rather than four in each pool, giving them ten matches rather than the current six. There are two possible ways to do this. One is to extend the European Cup from 20 teams to 24, with four groups of six. This would leave Wales with five or possibly six qualifiers, with the remaining top league teams going into the European Shield. The alternative to that would be to incorporate the Shield into the European Cup and go up to 48 teams, with eight groups of six. The group stages could be completed before Christmas, the later stages towards the end of the season. After Christmas, the domestic league, which could remain the same if the countries involved are happy with the arrangement, would be played. We should also retain the domestic cup competition. It adds excitement to the season and is good for the small clubs who get the chance to play the big names. I do not think it is too much to ask Swansea, Cardiff or Llanelli to play the occasional cup tie at somewhere like Trebanos, Senghenydd or Cefn Cribwr, where a visit by big-name players will help sustain clubs which might one day produce the next Rob Howley or Colin Charvis.

Some of you will have been adding up the total number of games through all this. A possible thirteen European Cup games, eight internationals, four or five cup games and perhaps eleven league games from a twelve-team competition, playing each other once, comes to around 37 games, one for each weekend between the start of September and mid-May – which is as long as you want the season to get. You will remember that I said top players should not play more than about thirty games a year, which still applies; this will encourage the clubs to bring on younger players on certain occasions. This in turn raises the question of how we should organise qualification for European competitions, and how far clubs will be willing to rest their best players if a European Cup place is on the line. If the cup were extended to 48 teams, there would be a place for everyone in the Premier League, so this would not be a problem. It would also guarantee some continuity, which would strengthen our prospects in the cup. If we stay at five or six teams, my suggestion is that perhaps three of those places should be allotted to the teams who have performed best in the previous season's European Cup. The other two or three could go to the highest-placed league teams.

The recruitment and retention of top Welsh players also raises a number of issues. The WRU's scheme of support payments to clubs with national squad players has helped bring players like Scott Quinnell back to Wales and stopped others from leaving. That helps the standard of Welsh club rugby, so it is welcome. But if a player wants to go and play in England and France he should not necessarily be discouraged. If he feels he will get a higher standard of play there – as John Scott and Maurice Colclough felt when they chose to play in Wales rather than England – that can work to Wales's benefit. Certainly we should not exclude anybody from national selection for doing so.

Similarly, we should not be too dogmatic about overseas players. Gary Teichmann, as I mentioned, has been superb for Newport. You don't ever want to exclude people like that. But before you import players you have to be sure that they do offer something extra, as Gary does. There are quite a few overseas players in Welsh rugby who offer little that you could not get from a local player, and are being paid quite a bit more into the bargain. If we are to develop our young players, the top Welsh clubs need to follow the example of a club like Neath, who almost invariably look around locally when they need a player. Swansea have an extremely good young hooker named Kevin Allen who is playing for Wales under-21s, but John Plumtree was not prepared to use him at senior level and went to New Zealand to get Greg Smith, the Fijian hooker – not a bad player, but certainly not a great player. He pushes Kevin another notch down the pecking order at a club that already has Garin Jenkins and Chris Wells on its books. It will almost certainly limit Kevin's chances and could hit Chris's as well. It is plain short-term thinking. Clubs should be putting their faith in young players and giving them the chance to develop.

Clubs also need to work on their pay structures to make them fairer. Having a few 'star' players on £100,000 or more when most are on salaries up to £30,000 is neither fair nor a particularly good way of building team spirit.

Most importantly of all, clubs need to look at the way players' time is being used. Being professional means players now have the time to work on all aspects of their game, and there is no doubt that players are now stronger and quicker than they were even five years ago. The best medical help is available immediately if you have a problem; ten years ago you might have had to wait until training on the Tuesday evening to speak to the physio about a problem you picked up on the Saturday. Yet I wonder if the best possible use is being made of the time. My view is that the vast majority of professional squads devote insufficient time to working on individual skills. A great deal of time is spent on defence, and much of the rest on set-piece coordination, fitness, power, organisation and team skills. All of these things are very important, and there is little doubt they are done much better than they were before. Yet they are not sufficient by themselves.

Working on skills should be part and parcel of the training week, something as ingrained as going to the gym or working on defensive organisation. Each position has specific skills players need to work on: a scrum-half might work on passing, kicking in defence and attack, perhaps ways of breaking from a set piece using simulated defences; an outside-half might work on passing, different types of kicking – the chip or grubber – and ways of beating people, practising his side-stepping; back rows now need to be able to pass as well as scrum-halves and occasionally have to kick, so need to practise. This does not mean you have to create a vast new wave of specialist coaches. Players should learn how to practise effectively by themselves, as ambitious players always used to do. Most clubs have ex-players who are more than willing to help out on occasion, if necessary. They don't have to have been better players than the current ones, just prepared to pass on their greater experience.

Coaching sessions need variety. The loudest cheers you are likely to hear at a training session erupt when a soccer ball comes out. It is a change in the routine, but it also serves a serious purpose: developing ball skills. We played a lot of touch rugby at Swansea in the 1980s. That develops your passing skills and your spatial awareness, teaches you how to avoid rather than run into opponents and hones your communication skills. It is the coaches who need to incorporate such work on individual skills into their structures, but there is also a responsibility on the players. My impression is that rather too many feel their job is done when they have finished their training sessions at the club, and are not working by themselves to develop skills. I realise that nowadays players may have two sessions five days a week, but I'm not saying that you must give up the whole of your free time to training. Just a couple of extra hours a week honing your ball skills will give a player an extra edge, making him that much more instinctive under pressure. I know my brother Rhodri works hard on his skills in his own time because he goes out with Dad two or three times a week and throws 150 passes or makes 100 kicks. He knows those skills are vital to his game. Arwel Thomas also does it; Neil Jenkins has always been the ultimate in dedication. I'm not sure how many other players apply themselves in this way.

Players who have developed their skills in these ways are the ones who know what to do when they find themselves in an unexpected situation – isolated on the field of play or put into a difficult position by a poor pass from a team-mate. They can adapt and think on their feet. You sometimes hear it argued that the players from the Wales teams of the 1970s would not cope today because modern players are so much stronger and quicker. That is missing the point completely. Outstanding players in any era are fit – it is a prerequisite for playing the game properly – but their attributes go far beyond fitness. They have the adaptability that comes from innate talent, instinct, vision and a desire to be the best.

Wales is at its best when it encourages those skills and the players who possess them; it loses its way when it loses confidence in them and instead starts trying to fit players into systems, rather than building systems around the talents of its best players. My own international career, lasting from 1986 to 1995, is to a great extent the story of how we lost confidence in our traditional virtues, lost our way and turned a team that should have been winning championships and Triple Crowns into one with an embarrassing collection of wooden spoons.

# 7 When the Going Was Good

'Everybody tells you that your first game goes by in a flash, and that's how it was for me. It was also disappointing. Nigel Melville was the opposing scrum-half – a terrific passer who never fulfilled his potential because he had so many injuries. He was always a strong opponent, but it was his half-back partner who made a real impression that day: we lost 21–18 to six penalties and a late drop goal from Rob Andrew. Beating Wales was a big thing for the English in those days. A couple of days later I put the television on, and there was Rob being interviewed on *Wogan*!'

Q UITE A FEW PEOPLE have argued that I was unlucky in my timing, because my career largely coincided with one of Welsh rugby's weaker periods. There is something in that, but in another respect my timing was extremely fortunate.

When I was growing up, Wales had outstanding scrum-halves. To start with there was Gareth Edwards, the player who had it all: the skills, the quick hands and feet, vision and incredible power. In a great era, he established himself as the dominant force in the game. I remember when my father told me that Gareth had retired. I became quite emotional as I realised that I wasn't going to see him play again.

Brynmor Williams, who had been Gareth's deputy at Cardiff and was a good enough player to have been chosen for the British Lions when he was not first choice at his club, was expected to be Gareth's successor. It did not happen for him. Brynmor, now one of the best, most perceptive news-paper commentators on Welsh rugby, particularly on back and scrum-half play, was overtaken at Cardiff and for Wales by Terry Holmes.

Terry, in his turn, became the dominant figure in Welsh rugby. He wasn't a classical scrum-half. He was somebody I could look at and admire, but not in the sense that I wanted to play the same way as him – that was obviously impossible. He did not have the greatest pass in the world, but there was so much else that was good about him. People talk about him as a physical player, and it is true he was big, very strong and lethal from a few yards out. But to talk about him simply in those terms is to misrepresent him. He had a very good rugby brain and knew his strengths and weaknesses. He scored a lot of tries, not just because he was strong at close quarters but because he ran exceptionally good lines of support and, in the same way as a good loose forward, was generally where he needed to be to carry on or finish off an attack. He was an extremely influential player, the obvious first choice when a Wales or a Lions team was being chosen.

My constant ambition when growing up was to play for Wales, but when I got into senior rugby in 1983 I concentrated on consolidating my place at Swansea. After a while I started thinking in terms of perhaps getting into the senior Wales squad, but there did not seem to be much prospect of actually playing while Terry was around. I knew there would be a chance eventually – he was eight and a half years ahead of me after all – but I had no idea that it would come so soon. He was still only 28 when, at the end of November 1985, he went off to join Bradford Northern. He had had quite a few injuries, received a good offer from rugby league and decided that he should cash in on his skills while he had the chance. People were genuinely shocked by his decision because he had been such a key figure in Welsh rugby.

It was my good fortune that he happened to go just as I was coming into the picture. I had already been talked about as a future Wales player. Ray Gravelle, who was doing quite a lot of broadcasting at that time, has always claimed that he was the first person to say in the media that I was going to play for Wales. He may well be right, but there were others saying the same sort of thing, like Ron Griffiths in the *Evening Post* and John Billot of the *Western Mail*, and Gerald Davies was always extremely supportive, which meant a great deal as he had been such a hero to me as a youngster.

The first hint that I might be coming into the selectors' minds came in October 1985, when I was still only nineteen. I was chosen for the Wales B team to play France in Sainte Foy le Grande. Paul Moriarty was in the side too, so his parents travelled across the Channel with mine. Geraint John was at outside-half and the other scrum-half in the squad was Carl Gnojek from Neath. Carl used to give me a bit of an earful when we played against them, calling me 'the little superstar', but he was a great bloke (if anything he was smaller than me, which made him a bit of a rarity). There was a beautiful playing surface at the French ground and they played a schoolboy match as a curtain-raiser. We were out watching it when all of a sudden one of the most spectacular brawls I have ever seen in my life broke out. It went on for several minutes, and there were spectators and coaches involved as well. I sat there on the side thinking, 'Bloody hell! I'm about to go and play against this lot – or at least their adult equivalents.'

We were well beaten, 30–13. I did not get the chance to do very much and came out feeling a little bit low and not at all sure I had had a good game. Then Barry John, who had been reporting on the game, came up to me and said, 'Well played. You really stood out.' Now a comment like that from somebody like Barry means an awful lot, particularly when you are at an early stage in your career. I found myself thinking that I must have played reasonably well if Barry thought so.

I was not named in the Wales squad for the November match against Fiji but, as I told the press at the time, I wasn't too disappointed because I wasn't really expecting it. I was still only nineteen, I had time on my side and Terry was still definitely the man in charge. Then, a few weeks later, Terry went north and the entire landscape changed.

The other top candidates to play at scrum-half – Mark Douglas, Ray Giles and David Bishop – were all different in style to me, all good players but much more physical. The possible advantage I had over them at the time was that Jonathan Davies had emerged at outside-half at the end of the previous season, and with his talents the priority had to be to get the ball to him as quickly as possible. Nevertheless, I told the papers at the time that I expected Ray Giles to be picked because he had already been involved in the Wales set-up, although as Brynmor had found out several years before that does not guarantee you anything.

I was included in the squad for the 1986 Five Nations along with Ray and Mark, but before the team to play England on 18 January was announced I had to play against Ray in the Whites' match at Aberavon. A lot of people began to set it up as a trial for the national scrum-half position, and things probably worked out in my favour. The game was played in horrendous conditions and was abandoned after 65 minutes with Aberavon leading 19–8. You might have expected that to favour Giloh's style of play, but he treated the match as a trial and spent the whole time trying to knock hell out of me. I concentrated on my game, moving the ball away quickly, and I must have made an impression.

The team was announced on the Friday after the Aberavon game. John Dawes, the coaching organiser, called me at work at John Morse solicitors. I did a couple of interviews, then my father took me back to Trebanos where we spent the evening in the Colliers pub. It was one of those evenings when all the village seemed to drop in to offer congratulations. Bleddyn Bowen, who had been selected as well, also dropped in for a while. All the family were there and it was a great night. I knew I would not be playing the following day against Newport – it was the tradition then that you withdrew the week before your first cap to avoid the risk of injury – and I got a marvellous reception at St Helen's the following day.

The national squad training sessions were on Sundays and Wednesdays at Waterton Cross, the South Wales Police ground at Bridgend, and come the day before the game we travelled up to London, staying just outside the city. The first ever Comic Relief programme was on that night, and I remember sitting up quite late with some of the lads watching it. I was rooming with Bleddyn. The idea was, presumably, that putting me in with the other Trebanos boy in the team would help to relax me. Fine in theory, but the trouble was that Bledd lived on his nerves before games. I think I probably spent more time calming him down. On the morning of the game he was sitting up in his pyjamas saying, 'This is going to be my last game. I can't stand the pressure.'

Everybody tells you that your first game goes by in a flash, and that's how it was for me. It was also disappointing. Nigel Melville was the opposing scrum-half – a terrific passer who never fulfilled his potential because he had so many injuries. He was always a strong opponent, but it was his half-back partner who made a real impression that day: we lost 21–18 to six penalties and a late drop goal from Rob Andrew. Beating Wales was a big thing for the English in those days. A couple of days later I put the television on, and there was Rob being interviewed on *Wogan*!

The evening after the game was memorable for different reasons. The new players – myself, John Devereux and David Waters, the lock forward who had missed his first cap the year before when he was chosen but matches were postponed – were presented with their caps before the dinner. Then I went to find Meg, who was then my girlfriend, and she was drunk. It was totally embarrassing. At one point she fell over and I tried to leave her, but someone came over and said, 'Is that your wife on the ground there?' There I was thinking, 'I'm the one who should be getting drunk, I've just had my first cap!' In fact I did not drink much at all, instead spending the whole night looking after Meg, who spent most of the coach journey back to Wales the following day asleep in the drivers' rest area. There was a reason for Meg's behaviour. Her father, Clive Rowlands, was on the selection committee and some people were saying that I had been chosen simply because I was going out with his daughter. People would say this to Meg's face, or ask her who had voted for whom, and she got very upset about it. It was something we had to get used to over the next couple of years, but at the time it was new to her and getting drunk was her way of soothing her bruised feelings.

So I had finally achieved my ambition and played for my country in a full international, but I still hadn't worn the red jersey at Cardiff Arms Park. I achieved that particular ambition a couple of weeks later when we played Scotland and beat them 22–15 in a match mainly remembered for Paul Thorburn's goalkicking, in particular an incredible penalty he landed from more than seventy yards out. The Scots scored three tries to our one, but Paul's kicking was the difference, just as Rob Andrew's had been a fortnight before. I was sharing a room with Jonathan this time. It was an extraordinary feeling to get up on the morning of the match and realise that four or five hours later I would be out on the Arms Park playing for Wales with more than 50,000 people shouting, screaming and singing for us.

For me, one of the best parts of the experience of playing in Cardiff happened before the game. On the Saturday morning I'd always go for a walk or a jog to loosen up. Some people wouldn't do anything on match day until they got to the ground, but I always took a while to get going so I'd go out to make sure I was properly wide awake. The bus journey into Cardiff was always another highlight. We would pass hundreds of Welsh supporters on their way to the match, every one of them cheering as they saw us. It made my hair stand on end. And there would always be people waiting for us when we arrived, perhaps as many as a hundred wanting autographs or simply wishing us luck. We would then walk down to the changing room, drop our bags there and go out on to the pitch. It would probably be a couple of hours before kick-off so there would only be a few thousand people in the ground, but there was always a response – and always people in the tunnel wanting things signed. Back in the changing rooms we'd find a couple of balls and start flicking them around. Perhaps I'd read the match programme too, maybe go and practise a few scrums and some passing with the forwards in the scrummaging pit.

It is hard to explain the feeling of that build-up, knowing that you will be out there playing for your country in a couple of hours, but that feeling never changed from my first cap to my fiftieth. The atmosphere and the tension build to the first whistle as the crowd noise grows, but as soon as the game starts you are so focused that you don't really notice the crowd. You are aware of the noise, but there is such a din that nothing specific comes through to you.

We went on to win in Ireland in February, but then lost to France in the last game of the season. They were too strong for us, as they were throughout my career. I was never on the winning side against France for Wales, although I did beat them with the Lions in 1989. Playing against them just felt different. Serge Blanco, for instance, was an extraordinary player – you never knew what he was going to do – and Philippe Sella always gave us trouble. Winning 111 caps shows enormous staying power. He was a superb tackler and had a very irritating habit of scoring against us. We were invariably confident against Ireland, Scotland and England – in the early days at least – thinking we were better than them and could beat them, but that confidence was never there against the French. We were rather in awe of them because we knew their record against us was so good. Pierre Berbizier was always one of the opponents I admired most. He was not the world's most gifted rugby player, but he was enormously effective because he had such an influence on everyone around him. France seem to have this ability to produce little men who are real leaders – Jacques Fouroux was another one. Perhaps it is something to do with Napoleon.

Indeed, the results of my first two Five Nations playing for Wales did not look anything special. After winning two matches out of four in 1986, we won only one, 19–12 against England, in 1987 and lost at home to Ireland seven weeks before we were due to play them in our opening match in the first ever World Cup. We took a lot of criticism in Wales. Expectations were still dictated by the great years of the 1970s, so winning one or two matches a season was not regarded as good enough.

Yet we had a real sense of something special developing. We had a young team, with players like Paul Moriarty, Bleddyn, Jonathan, John Devereux, Phil Davies and Adrian

Hadley. They all played in 1986, and the following year Ieuan Evans was capped for the first time, Stuart Evans came back into the team at prop and Bob Norster, a world-class lock forward, returned to the team after missing the 1986 Five Nations. When John Devereux was injured in 1987, Mark Ring had a chance to come back in, so we had real depth of quality at centre.

Meanwhile, I was developing my half-back relationship with Jonathan. We were good at taking pressure off each other, taking responsibility when there were problems. At this stage of our careers I saw my job as a simple one: to get the ball to Jonathan as quickly as possible so that he could work his magic. Jonathan was inspirational, and his confidence infected the other players. His brilliance created opportunities for those outside him because opponents concentrated so strongly on him. They were terrified of what he might do to them, and had good reason to be. He could destroy any opposition, as he showed in the 1986 New South Wales World Sevens tournament when he beat the All Blacks just about single-handedly, scoring a hat-trick. The All Blacks, who went on to win the tournament, had no idea what to do with him. In terms of sheer talent, he was head and shoulders above anybody else in the competition. We got to the semi-final before losing narrowly to Australia, and enjoyed a fair amount of success in sevens tournaments during this period – although my best achievement was not for Wales at all. In one tournament where we had been knocked out, Scotland ran short of players due to injuries. Paul Moriarty and myself were recruited as honorary Scotsmen, and we reached the final. Finlay Calder was the captain – we learned something along the way about the Scottish talent for inspirational ranting!

So we were confident that the team was going the right way, whatever our results and critics might indicate. We believed in each other and in our talent as a team. And we had complete confidence in and respect for our coach, Tony Gray, and assistant coach, Derek Quinnell. They did a terrific job, a fact which was not fully appreciated at the time. There was nothing terribly innovative about the way they operated, but it suited us perfectly.

Tony, like any coach at the time, had only a limited time with us and he was sensible enough to realise that this placed restrictions on what he could do. He offered a degree of organisation, but much more importantly he encouraged players to express themselves and do what they were good at. The reason why we had been chosen for Wales in the first place was that we were regarded as having certain abilities. Tony was not the sort of coach who then tried to turn you into something else; he allowed us to be ourselves within a team context. Both Tony and Derek understood that you get the best out of Welsh players by allowing them to express themselves. We also had players, like Jonathan, Bleddyn and Mark Ring, who had the skills to make this style of play work. You could talk and joke with Tony and Derek; they were always approachable. The lines you never heard from Tony were 'this is how you are going to play' or 'we did not tell you to play that way'. The way we played emerged from discussions between Tony and all fifteen players. Everyone had an input. They were there to provide guidance and advice, but we all had a part in it. This attitude won them a lot of respect from the players, which at the 1987 World Cup and in the 1988 Five Nations translated into good results.

Our relationship with them and among ourselves was already healthy by the 1986 tour of the South Pacific, which at the time was a real adventure. The three countries we visited were not yet fully recognised rugby nations – we knew a little bit about Fiji, but Tonga had been over to Britain only once and we knew nothing at all about Western Samoa (given our experiences at their hands since, some people in Wales would rather things had stayed that way!). It turned out to be an immensely demanding tour, not just because of the distances we had to travel but because of the physical nature of some of the rugby played there and the conditions we encountered. But because it was so tough, we came together as a squad.

We won the test match against Fiji in Suva on the last day of May, but David Pickering was badly injured. He was tackled, and as he went down somebody stood on his head. He was out cold, and when he came round he started going into fits. We hardly saw Dai, who was the captain of the team, after that, although he did not go home for about a week. He just stayed in his room. He came back as captain the following season, but he was never really the same force again and was dropped before the end of the 1987 Five Nations.

Richard Moriarty took over as captain, an excellent choice as he was hugely respected by all the players, and in June we moved on to Tonga. The accommodation in Fiji had been good, and from the photos we had seen we were expecting the International Dateline Hotel in Tonga to be of a similar standard. Instead, the country was like nowhere any of us had seen before. There were no roads or streetlights outside and rats ran across the shelves in the duty-free shop. There was no television on the island, and the radio station seemed to broadcast one record and one news bulletin every day. The place was also full of transvestites who were rather more interested in us than we would have liked. Adrian Hadley, a big, strong lad who stood very little nonsense, became a sort of minder for us, physically throwing them out if they became a problem.

The test match was lively even before it kicked off. The changing room, which was so tiny that we changed in the hotel, had vented windows, and while we were warming up Stuart Evans smashed one of them. The police wanted to arrest him, and Tony and Derek had to work very hard to persuade them to wait until after the game before doing anything about it.

The match itself was extraordinary. About fifteen minutes in the worst brawl I have ever seen on a rugby field – much worse than the punch-up in France the year before – broke out. Most punch-ups last about ten seconds; this must have lasted for a good minute and a half. I got involved when I went in to help Mark Brown who had been punched to the floor by three Tongan forwards and was being kicked. The only people not involved were Malcolm Dacey and Mark Titley who were on the halfway line watching in disbelief. The only one of us who was getting much out of it was John Devereux, who was knocking lumps out of his immediate opponent. Tonga had this prop called Tevita Bloomfield who had played against Wales at the Arms Park in 1975, and he took on about three or four people. Stuart Evans, Billy James and Adrian Hadley, all hard men, were down, and Adrian was out cold. He then started chasing Bleddyn Bowen who ran for cover into the crowd, and they threw him out! In the end they had to get an ambulance, which came over the pitch towards Adrian. It is about the only time I have ever felt frightened on a rugby field. If Richard Moriarty had said, 'Right, that's it, we're going off,' I would have been the first person into the dressing room. There was a recording of the match and we had every intention of passing it on to the International Rugby Board, but it mysteriously disappeared from BBC Wales commentator Huw Llewellyn Davies's bag.

Still, we won the match 15–7 and had a sort of revenge at the after-match dinner. They asked for a speech in Welsh. Our manager, George Morgan, did not speak Welsh, so Jonathan, who speaks Welsh and was the biggest name in the party, was called up. He was supposed to relay what George and Tony Gray had said in their speeches. What he was actually saying, although with a lot more expletives, was: 'This is the worst place I have ever been to. They call it Paradise Island, but it is a shithole. I am delighted to be leaving and I never want to come here again. You are the dirtiest team I have ever played against.' The Tongans were all clapping and laughing. Anyone who saw the curry-house scene in the film *Twin Town* will know what it was like.

Samoa came as something of a relief after that. We won the test match handsomely, 32–14, against a team including Michael Jones, who was only twenty but was already an excellent loose forward. Dick Moriarty did an excellent job as captain, and it was a memorable tour for another Swansea team-mate, Malcolm Dacey. We'd been having problems at full-back and Malcolm, who played outside-half for Swansea, changed position with complete comfort and assurance. It illustrated the point that good players with real footballing skills can change position perfectly happily, provided they have the attributes necessary for the position. Malcolm also kicked goals on the tour. He hardly ever played full-back or kicked goals for Swansea because Mark Wyatt did both jobs very well for us, but when the need arose on a tough international tour he did both with aplomb.

Part of the idea behind the South Pacific tour was to prepare us for the 1987 World Cup. That was something of a journey into the unknown as well. It was the inaugural World Cup, so nobody knew how well the idea would succeed, although I think by the end of the first series of matches everybody knew this was something that was here to stay for good. It was on a much smaller scale than more recent World Cups, with much less publicity and smaller crowds, but there was no doubt that it was a success. We felt we contributed a fair amount to that success by reaching the semi-final and coming third, but we did not get full credit for it. The reason was the 49–6 hammering we took from New Zealand in the semi-final, which tended to blot out memories of the five matches we won, including that third-place match against Australia. But we did very well to get to the semi-final. Nobody had expected us to make it.

We started in Wellington on 25 May against Ireland, who had beaten us less than two months earlier at Cardiff in the Five Nations, and disposed of them surprisingly comfortably, 13–6. After that we were expected to get to the quarter-finals, but we still had a couple of matches to get through, the first of those against the Tongans on 29 May. We did not play well, possibly because a lot of us had played against them the year before and were a little apprehensive. It was pretty physical again, and it is never easy to play rugby knowing you are going to be battered if you hang on to the ball. Glen Webbe, however, scored a hat-trick, of which the third was remark-able. He had been badly concussed by a tackle from the Tongan full-back, who was flying in with head-high tackles on everyone (a year or so later we heard that he had lost his arm in a machete attack). It was a superb solo try, but when we went to congratulate him as he ran back from scoring, he genuinely did not know what he had done. I set up one of the tries for Adrian Hadley by chipping through to him, but not all our back moves worked as well. A move involving Malcolm Dacey and Paul Thorburn certainly didn't, and they collided a couple of times, spilling the ball.

Still, we won 29–16 and gave a few of our squad a run-out into the bargain – something we continued to do in the final group match against Canada. This was pretty physical as well – a bit too physical at times, as when Ray Giles, who played instead of me at scrum-half, punched their scrum-half Ian Stuart (it was a good punch too: Stuart, an excellent player who later appeared at centre, had to have about a dozen stitches and some people thought Gilesy was lucky to stay on). We were never likely to lose to Canada, but we took a long time to make certain of the victory, Ieuan having a great afternoon scoring four tries.

We were not expected to beat England in the quarter-final on 8 June, perhaps because we had looked so ordinary against Tonga, but we felt confident and we won convincing-ly, 16–3. I scored my first try for Wales, kicking through and beating Richard Harding, the England scrum-half, to the touchdown. It had taken a while coming – it was my fourteenth international – but I hoped that once I had got one, they would come a little more frequently. Little did I know! I was never very concerned about try-scoring myself; it only bothered me when other people raised the issue or suggested that I couldn't be playing well because I was not scoring that often. It was far more important to me that Wales won and I produced a good all-round performance.

That win over England took us through to the semi-final against New Zealand in Brisbane on 14 June. We knew New

Zealand were a good team – they had beaten Scotland by thirty points in the quarter-final, and Scotland had not played badly – yet we had no idea what was about to happen to us. We honestly thought we could beat them in a one-off match. We had won four matches in a row, were feeling confident and had a pretty good back line. One problem was that we had a lot of injuries, particularly in the forwards. Stuart Evans, Billy James, Gareth Roberts and Bob Norster were all missing. If we had a problem as a squad, it was a slight lack of depth. The replacements were not bad players, and they tried very hard, but they were inexperienced players up against people like the Whetton brothers, Wayne Shelford and Michael Jones.

It is an extraordinary experience to play against a team which is so much better than you. Within a couple of minutes we were in awe of them. They were so dominant in every phase of the game. They had everything: they were strong in the scrum, in the ruck and maul, strong and skilful in the backs and up front. People talked about them having an ordinary back division, but every player in that team did their job: Grant Fox was an extraordinary goalkicker, John Kirwan was a great finisher, John Gallagher was on his way to being the best full-back in the world. We were simply over-whelmed. Our scrum was going backwards from the start, and we won very little possession. Coaches always talked about 'playing for eighty minutes', and these All Blacks came closer to doing it than any team I ever played against. They never let up. The concept of ball retention has only become popular in the last nine or ten years, but they were brilliant at it back in 1987. There were hardly any basic errors or loose passes. If you made a mistake, it was punished. And they were just as committed to making sure we did not score. I remember one occasion when Ieuan got away down the wing. New Zealand had a huge lead by then, but Kirwan still came charging across the field, as though he were protecting a one-point lead. They were professional in attitude and standards of organisation while the rest of the game was still amateur.

Family ties. At home in Trebanos with (from left to right) my father and mother, Tiaan, Emily, Margaret and Clive, and Meg.

He ain't heavy, he's my brother. In club colours with Ant (left, South Wales Police) and Rhod (centre, Neath).

*Left* Mascot duty. Emily is carried off the pitch at St Helens by her proud uncle Rhod.

*Right* Starting out. Getting a pass away against Newport in my first season as Richie Collins closes in.

*Below* The Trebanos boys. As well as playing rugby for Wales, Arwel Thomas (left), Bleddyn Bowen (centre) and myself all played cricket for Pontardawe CC.

*Above* Winners at last. Lifting the SWALEC Cup after Swansea's win in 1995.

*Below* Meeting Princess Diana. Mike Rayner (centre) and Neil Jenkins (right) look suitably impressed.

*Above* Not the Kelly gang. It wasn't all misery in Australia in 1991! With me are (from left to right) Richard Webster, Scott Gibbs and Anthony Clement.

*Below* Under pressure. Left isolated for once for the Lions against Australia in 1989.

"He's changed his mind again — today he wants Robert Jones to run the country"

Floating voter. While we were in New Zealand and Australia for the 1987 World Cup, it was election time back home.

*Right* Three points to Pontypridd. Neil Jenkins, a great player not always appreciated or used properly.
(© John Harris)

*Below* They don't make hairstyles like that any more. With (from left to right) Jonathan Davies, Bleddyn Bowen and John Devereux at the 1987 World Cup.

Through the gap. On the break against England, as Rob Andrew (left) tries to cover.
(© John Harris)

Quick service. Although Aled Williams (right) evidently wonders where it is going!
(© John Harris)

They scored two quick tries and just kept on coming at us. We did not play that well – you don't when you are overwhelmed – nor did we always help ourselves. Our lock forward Huw Richards was sent off, even though in order to be sent off he had to be brought round after being laid out by a retaliatory punch from Buck Shelford. John Devereux, who had a terrific World Cup, scored our try, but we were taken apart. It is not the sort of game which makes for happy memories. In one sense you would rather forget it, but it was also something to appreciate, just to have been on the same field as such a great side. It is odd that that fifteen is not mentioned more often when great teams are discussed, because as far as I'm concerned they were the best side I ever played against. If you could bring them back now as the team they were in 1987 and expose them to modern training methods and diets, they would be as good as anybody, quite possibly better.

It was after this game that my father-in-law and our manager Clive Rowlands was asked, 'Where does Welsh rugby go from here?' Clive answered, 'Back to beating England every year.' It was not the wisest thing Clive has ever said, and he has had it thrown back at him on countless occasions in the years since, although it should be pointed out in his defence that we did go on doing it for a while.

Clive's chirpy answer concealed the squad's devastation. What do you do after an experience like that? We did what rugby teams of the time did under those circumstances: we went out on the beer and had one hell of a night. A group of us ended up drinking with the footballer Bryan Robson, who was in Australia for a charity game. Rugby players are supposed to be able to drink, but I have never seen anyone like Bryan. We ended up drinking in shifts with him. I went to bed at about three, and Bleddyn woke me about an hour later and told me it was my turn to go back to drink with him. All of us took at least an hour off, and Bryan was still there at seven in the morning – ridiculously drunk, but so were the rest of us.

It was not what a dietician or a fitness specialist would recommend, but it did us all a lot of good. We enjoyed being out with Bryan and it got the experience of being hammered by the All Blacks out of our system quickly. That was important, because we still had one game to go – the third-place match against Australia, who had lost an incredible semi-final against France in Rotorua. Our initial reaction was that we could not see why we had to play this game. We wanted to go home. But we soon realised that this was our chance to redeem ourselves and show we could still play. The feeling of 'let's pull together and show them' brought us all closer as a squad.

The atmosphere was great in the days leading up to the game, then we flew to Rotorua where we found a superb playing surface and 30,000 New Zealanders who had decided they were Welsh for the day and gave us fantastic support. I know Australia had David Codey sent off in the first few minutes and it still took us until the dying minutes to win the match – Adrian Hadley went over in the corner and Paul Thorburn kicked a great conversion from near the touchline – but it can often be tough to win against fourteen men and Australia were a good side, especially in defence. We had had to lift ourselves from a devastating experience the previous weekend, too.

From the atmosphere in the changing room afterwards you would have thought that we had won the World Cup, not come third. We felt proud of that achievement, and felt we did not get the credit we deserved. All the comments afterwards were about how other teams had played better and we were lucky to be third. The five matches we had won were forgotten and all the talk was about the defeat by New Zealand. But the negativity helped us in one way: it took us into the following season with a point to prove.

Personally, the 1987 World Cup was one of the best experiences of my career; the games against Tonga, England and Australia were among the best I played for Wales. After the first couple of matches in the tournament there were comments in the New Zealand press along the lines of: 'We knew all about Jonathan Davies, but the guy playing inside him who we didn't know about is the one who gets them going.' I was beginning to be talked about as one of the best scrum-halves in the world. After you get picked for Wales, your next ambitions are to play for the Lions and to be regarded as the best in the world, and it was good to be talked about in those terms. In November I was voted the best European player in the World Cup; I had been nominated as the best Welsh player the month before. I was delighted to finish ahead of players like Pierre Berbizier and Gavin Hastings, both of whom had had great tournaments.

Mind you, not everyone in Wales was so convinced. David Bishop was playing brilliantly for Pontypool and a campaign was started by the papers in Gwent to get David into the Wales side. I did my best not to take it personally; after all, David was a hugely talented player. He was strong, dynamic and was confident in a way most Welsh people are not. He might have been a top player in any number of positions, and perhaps I was lucky that the Wales selectors were always worried about his character, so he only got the one cap. But it did all get rather silly that 1987/8 season when Swansea played Pontypool in the cup. They beat us in the mud, and David had a terrific game, finishing things off by kicking a couple of penalties. As we walked off people were shouting at me; I was spat at and a woman tried to hit me with her umbrella. Later on I was having a drink with David in the bar when a spectator came up and wanted to fight me. David told him to forget about it. The Pontypool committee were also very good about it and extremely apologetic.

Fortunately, the Wales team was not being selected by the *South Wales Argus*, and I was still in it for the 1988 Five Nations, when we won a Triple Crown and should have taken the Grand Slam as well. Bleddyn had been made captain and was ideal for the job. In spite of the nerves, which stopped as soon as he got on to the field, he enjoyed taking responsibility. Even Jonathan needed help and reassurance on occasion, and he would always look to Bleddyn, whom he looked up to. Bleddyn had a relaxed style as captain. He was not the sort of leader who has to be in control of everything and we would all have our say, but when it was necessary to pull together and make a decision you knew he was in charge.

There was controversy over the team to play England in the first match at Twickenham on 6 February when Tony Clement was chosen instead of Paul Thorburn at full-back. It was tough luck on Thorby. He wasn't the greatest attacking full-back in the world, but he was an incredible goalkicker and particularly good in a crisis, as he had shown with that conversion against Australia in Rotorua, and as he would show again in Dublin in the first week in March. Tony Clement played outside me at outside-half for Swansea, but Tony and Derek had the foresight to realise that he was exactly what Wales needed at full-back. He could do the basics of the full-back's defensive duties – he was a good tackler and an excellent kicker who could make huge distances – and he brought a fresh dimension to our attacking play with his pace, good angles and ability to beat people. It was hard on Thorby, but it was an advance in the way we wanted to play.

Tony was a revelation in a terrific match at Twickenham which we won 11–3 with two great long-range team tries finished by Adrian Hadley, the first of which started when Tony took the ball in our 25 and went off on a run. He went past three or four tacklers and passed to Bleddyn who carried on the move. When he offloaded, Wade Dooley tried to intercept it. I went for it at the same time and somehow got it – Dooley was probably as surprised as I was because he was about a foot taller than me and a lot heavier – and we scored after an eighty-yard movement during which about half a dozen people handled with some lovely work by Tony and Mark Ring before Adrian went over.

The evening after the game was on the lively side as well. The dinner was at the Hilton, but about halfway through a few of us went over to the bar where we found quite a few of the English lads. Staff Jones, our prop forward from Ponty-pool, was propping up the bar – or possibly it was the other way round. Staff was normally pretty quiet, but this changed after he had had a few drinks, and that night he was very drunk. To start with he was standing at the end of the bar, but then he decided to run up and scrummage everyone who was at the bar against the far wall. Staff, who spent his working life swinging a sledgehammer as a colliery surface worker, was incredibly strong, and he soon had about half a dozen people driven up against the wall, all trying to get away from him. Then he decided to tackle Johnny Price, the London Welsh representative who was going around getting signatures on a rugby ball. Not a gentle tackle, but the sort you'd put in in a game, which drove poor Johnny, who must have been seventy, into the floor. He nearly had a heart attack.

In our next match, at Cardiff on 20 February, we beat Scotland after going ten points down, which was a huge margin in those days. Scotland were always tough opposition, particularly John Jeffrey. Their back rows always put you under pressure, pushing the limits of the offside law and getting away with more than most (when you drive into Edinburgh from the airport, the road signs say 'Offside for Murrayfield', so they obviously still remember John!). But we never stopped believing in ourselves and it was one of those days when Jonathan seemed to be able to do anything: he scored a solo try from my interesting pass and dropped a couple of goals. Ieuan scored an incredible try as well, cutting in from the wing and side-stepping past four or five defenders. He was already an exceptional player. He wasn't that big, but he was very strong around the hips and had real explosive power. He was also an excellent defender who would back himself to stop anybody, closing them down so quickly that they ran out of options. He wasn't the greatest trainer in those days, though – the real self-discipline came later when he was captain of Wales – so he carried a little extra weight, but he was already an incredible finisher and head and shoulders above every other right-wing in Wales.

The Ireland match a fortnight later was different, one of those afternoons when the Irish come at you at a hundred miles an hour and you have to dig really deep to cope with them. The Irish were really fired up. On one occasion I fell on the ball near our line and wound up at the bottom of a ruck. Philip Matthews stamped on me and split my ear open. The irony was that, with Willie Anderson, he was my closest friend among the Irish players. We got on really well, especially when we met up to play for the Barbarians. It was a spur-of-the-moment thing, and Philip was enormously apologetic about it afterwards. Still, our 12–9 win was a pleasing one because after showing a lot of skill to win the first two matches, we needed real character to win this one. Thorby, who had come back into the side because Tony was injured and was an ideal man to have around in a close match, coolly kicked the penalty that gave us our first Triple Crown for nine years.

It should have been a Grand Slam and a championship as well. We played France in Cardiff on 19 March and had enough possession to win the match, but I have to hold my hand up, and I expect Jonathan would as well, and say that we did not play well. We have to accept the responsibility for losing by a single point that horrible, wet day. My service was not good enough, my confidence was hit a bit and we did not take the right decisions. There was a glorious Grand Slam for the taking, and we failed.

Even so, we went on the summer tour of New Zealand in a positive frame of mind, although there was a school of thought that another South Pacific adventure might be better for building up a little more confidence and continuity. We were not sure we were quite ready for New Zealand, particularly in the middle of an itinerary that threw us straight in against some of their top provincial sides, but we had no doubt we had improved a great deal since the World Cup and could at least give them a decent game. The trouble was that they had improved as well. After trouncing us they had gone on to win the World Cup, and basically the same team had stayed together for another year and got even stronger and more confident. Nobody could live with them – they were about to go to Australia and put thirty points on them in two games out of three.

We struggled from the start, losing when we should have beaten Waikato and then taking a terrible hammering against Wellington for whom Hika Reid, who could not get into the All Blacks side, was awesome. We just beat Otago, then went into the first test at Lancaster Park on 28 May. It was the World Cup semi-final all over again, and we were massacred 52–3. They were outstanding, completely unstoppable.

The other scrum-half on the tour was Jonathan Griffiths from Llanelli who had come through very strongly in the year since the World Cup. He was very strong, more physical than me and extremely quick – I did not realise quite how quick until I trained with him. He was playing extremely well on tour and had an excellent game against North Auckland just before the second test, in spite of the fact that the team as a whole played very badly. One of the papers gave Phil May a mark of none out of ten. Nobody is that bad, but it made the point that we really did not compete. So I knew I was under pressure for my place in the second test, and was half expecting the phone call I received in my room. It was Rod Morgan, the chairman of selectors, who said, 'Come and have a chat.' He told me that the selectors had decided to go with Jonathan Griffiths as they felt they needed more physical presence.

I appreciated the fact that they had taken the trouble to explain the decision to me, and it was the right decision. My confidence was low and I had not been playing well. Jonathan, on the other hand, was playing well, and he was the right option for the second test. But it was still the most devastating moment of my rugby career. I walked out of the room and burst into tears. In fact, I was embarrassingly tearful; Phil May and a couple of the boys had to take me out for a couple of drinks to console me. It was the first time I had ever been dropped. It was an experience that was to become all too familiar later in my career – and it was rarely handled as well as it was this first time – but later on I was more mature and had some experience of suffering emotional disappointment. This time it was new to me, and I was shell-shocked.

I hurled myself into the next training session. It was strange being part of the opposition in preparation for an international; I was so used to being part of the team. But the adrenalin was flowing and I was determined to show that I was part of the squad and not to let my disappointment get in the way of helping to prepare the team for another encounter with the All Blacks. But all our work was in vain; we were thrashed again, 54–9. Jonathan Davies had a magnificent game, scoring our try, but we were hopelessly outclassed.

When we returned to Wales, Tony Gray and Derek Quinnell were sacked. It was a crazy decision which did far more damage than the defeats at the hands of the All Blacks. Wales certainly did not recover from the shock of it during my career. Tony and Derek had complete respect and support from a talented group of players who were developing well. There was cohesion within the squad. When I meet other players from that period I am reminded of the regard we had for each other – you are forever hearing that other members of the team were great players or a pleasure to play alongside. The Welsh Rugby Union were hypnotised by those three hefty defeats by New Zealand, to the exclusion of all else. They set up a committee of inquiry full of people who had not been to New Zealand and who therefore could never understand quite how good a side they were. Jonathan offered to sit on the inquiry and put the players' point of view, but he was told 'no thank you'.

In the year up to the summer of 1988 we had finished third in the World Cup and won a Triple Crown. Since then we have not beaten a traditional rugby nation in three World Cups, two of them at home, and have not won a single Triple

Crown. We were not as good as New Zealand in the late 1980s, but nor was anybody else. We were, however, as good as anybody in Europe. I believe we would have won a Grand Slam in 1989 and gone on to be serious challengers for several years but for the WRU's knee-jerk reaction. England had one of the best teams in their history in the early 1990s, but I believe we could have competed with them. Instead they stole a march on us, and we have never really caught up.

Furthermore, had Derek and Tony kept their jobs and Welsh rugby stayed strong, we would not have suffered the losses to rugby league that occurred over the next couple of years. Jonathan received an extremely good offer from Widnes that would have been hard to refuse at any time, so he did not go simply because he was upset at the way Derek and Tony had been treated, but I do know how disappointed he was at what happened to them and it meant that he was far more receptive than he would otherwise have been when the offer came. Remember, one of Jonathan's greatest ambitions was to be a British Lion, and he went to Widnes only a few months before the 1989 tour of Australia, for which he would have been a certain selection. Had Derek and Tony still been in charge, and had Jonathan felt more certain about the future of top-flight rugby union in Wales, I don't believe he would have gone.

There are a lot of possible reasons why Welsh rugby has been in decline over the last twenty years or so. There has been great social change in Wales. The coal industry has gone, steel is going the same way and there have been big changes in public services like teaching and the police, which traditionally supplied a lot of players to top-class rugby. There have been reorganisations in schools. People argue about the impact these changes have had on the game, and frequently disagree. And they are all completely outside the control of the Welsh Rugby Union. They have to live with the consequences, having had no influence over the causes.

But some of the problems have been self-inflicted, and were entirely avoidable. In my opinion, the sacking of Derek

Quinnell and Tony Gray was the worst single decision – and there's some strong competition for that accolade – the WRU took during my career as a player. Things were never really the same again.

# 8 Losing Our Way

'Everyone remembers the way things fell apart on the Australia tour, but the truth is that what happened there was merely the culmination of divisions and frustrations that had built up over the previous eighteen months. We were suffering from a national identity crisis. We weren't Wales any more, united in our desire to do well for our country. That is not to say we did not want to do well, but the divisions were so deep we felt disabled.'

E VERYONE PAID FOR THE LUDICROUS PANIC of the Welsh Rugby
Union in sacking Tony Gray and Derek Quinnell. It was
a particular blow to the players. For a start, we had to
adjust to a new style of coaching, in place of one we knew and
trusted. Then, as is normal when you see coaches fired in that
way, you are bound to think, 'Could I be next?' It had a serious,
inhibiting effect on our confidence as a group. The union and
Welsh rugby fans suffered too when what should have been a
period of success became one of almost non-stop struggle.

Unlike a cricketer or baseball player, a rugby player doesn't
have many detailed statistics to back up any debate about
how well he is playing, but statistics for Wales performances
are available, and those during my career tell a clear story.
The last match I played under Tony and Derek was the first
test in Christchurch on 28 May 1988. At the end of it I had 22
caps. Wales had won fourteen of those matches, including
five in the World Cup and three to complete the 1988 Triple
Crown. Of the remaining 31 matches I was to start between
the winter of 1988 and my final cap at the 1995 World Cup,
Wales lost 25. I had played in twelve Five Nations matches up
to the end of the 1988 campaign, winning six and losing six.
That was not regarded as a very good record in Wales, but it
was a great deal better than what was to come over the next
seven seasons. In that time I started twenty Five Nations
matches for my country and won four of them.

One reason why we played so badly was instability in
coaching, leading to constant changes in style. The team lost

confidence and cohesion as it tried to adjust to the changes. When Kevin Bowring became national coach in autumn 1995 he was the fifth national coach in just over seven years. The timing of the changes was nearly always bad. We went into both the 1991 and the 1995 World Cups with new coaches, brought in at short notice. There was another change mid-season in 1990, forcing another quick fix. It would be easy to blame the coaches themselves for what happened, but unfair. They also had to cope with uncertainty and insecurity.

John Ryan, Ron Waldron and Alan Davies were all men of integrity, decent men who were desperate to achieve success for Wales and went about it in ways they were convinced were right. They all brought good records to the job, too: John from the Wales under-21 team, Ron from making Neath into the dominant club side in Wales and Alan from Nottingham and his time in the England set-up. Alan, in particular, was an outstanding coach, but I felt that all of them had a piece of the jigsaw we needed to build strongly. John was organised and analytical. I have never known anyone with a more passionate will to win than Ron. Alan restored stability and intelligence to our game and, with Bob Norster and Gareth Jenkins, brought back something of the atmosphere we had under Tony and Derek. If you could have brought together the best qualities of John, Ron and Alan, you would have been somewhere close to an ideal.

But, as I said, it was never easy for them. We lost many of our best players to rugby league during this period. Jonathan was the best-known of the code-changers and the greatest blow to our confidence and ability to play the way we wanted to. But there were plenty of other losses. We struggled consistently to generate decent possession through this period, for instance, and I doubt those problems would have been as acute had we not lost two exceptional prop forwards, Stuart Evans and David Young, to rugby league. Paul Moriarty and John Devereux also went when they were out of favour, meaning that they played probably their best years in league rather than for Wales. Adrian Hadley had made a habit of scoring vital tries for us, such as the winner in the third-place match in the 1987 World Cup and the two at Twickenham in 1988. All of them went in the space of a couple of years, and there were to be further losses as we moved into the 1990s: Rowland Phillips, Allan Bateman, Scott Gibbs, Richard Webster and Scott Quinnell.

Injury played its part too. We lost Bob Norster, our outstanding ball-winner, after 1989. Mark Ring was also lost. You cannot do much about that, but Bleddyn Bowen, Mark's partner in the outstanding centre pairing in our Triple Crown team, was discarded when he still had a great deal to offer. Those of us who were left were often short on confidence or divided as a squad. We went to Australia in 1991 and to the World Cup in 1995 as hopelessly divided teams, unsure of our identity. On both occasions an attempt was made to base the national team on a single club and its playing style, but this simply alienated players from other clubs. Making that mistake once might be understandable; doing it twice is hard to believe.

It was all so unnecessary, and could have been avoided if the WRU had kept faith with Tony Gray and Derek Quinnell. That is not to say that there would not have been changes. No doubt new players would have come through and others would have lost form or been injured. But I have no doubt we would have retained essentially the same squad, and would have done well with it.

Instead, the WRU sacked them and put John Ryan into their place. John had done very well with the Wales under-21 team and, although he came from Gwent, had the advantage of not being particularly associated with any club. Not having baggage of that sort can be a great help in Wales, as Graham Henry has demonstrated. John was a thoroughly nice guy, very laid back. We struck up a particularly good rapport when we went out to the World Sevens in Australia in 1989, and I became captain of Wales, a lifelong ambition of mine, in 1990 while John was coach. But his time in charge was not particularly happy for me or the team.

When Derek and Tony put up an idea and two or three of us thought it would not work, they were always prepared to listen and reconsider; John's style was much more rigid and regimented, concerned with doing what the coach thought we should do. He anticipated some of the methods of modern coaching. It was under him, for instance, that I saw flipcharts being used for the first time. He also introduced the idea of the field being divided into three sections: defence, build and attack. In the defensive third of the field we would kick or drive from a line-out, in the midfield we would build opportunities and in the final third we were allowed to be ourselves and be creative again. John argued that there was little point in advancing thirty yards by handling the ball through several phases which could take quite a while when a kick would get you there in a moment. You could see the logic in this, but it limited and inhibited the way we played. There were literally dozens of options to remember. Going to a set piece – say, a line-out – when you should have been thinking, 'We want ball straight off the top here because Jonathan wants it', you would be thinking, 'Right, we've got a line-out in midfield, about ten yards into their half. What was the drill again?' It reduced initiative and made us less natural and instinctive in our play.

There was a revealing moment quite early in John's period in charge, in camp in Portugal. Nigel Davies, who had won his first cap in John's first game – against Western Samoa in November 1988 – asked, 'What if we get the ball in our 22 and there's space to run it back?' John replied, 'You can run it back if you want to, but if you cock it up it will be your last game for Wales.' It was intended to be funny, but at the time, with a team feeling insecure about the way it ought to be playing, it rather hit home.

John's humour was never ill-intentioned – he was not that sort of person – but it was not always well timed. Bleddyn Bowen soon got back into the squad after a period out with an injury, and John said to him, 'So you're back again. I thought I'd got rid of you once before.' It was intended to be humorous, but Bledd was not feeling terribly confident and he rather took it to heart. The games against Scotland and Ireland in the 1989 Five Nations were the last Bleddyn played for his country. He was only 27 and he still had a huge amount to offer us. You may think it local bias when I say what a good player he was, but you don't have to take my word for it. Ask Jonathan, John Devereux, Mark Ring or any of the people who played with Bleddyn for Wales. They will say exactly the same.

We particularly needed Bleddyn because we had lost Jonathan to rugby league after the defeat by Romania in Cardiff on 10 December 1988. Romania were big and strong and put us under pressure up front, but we should still have been able to beat them. We were better and more skilful than them, but we lacked the confidence to play with any freedom. As soon as they put pressure on us, we were on the back foot, with no belief in our ability to play our way out of trouble. That performance was the direct outcome of what had built up over the previous seven months – not just what had happened in New Zealand, but all the changes since. We had stopped thinking for ourselves on the rugby field. We were just trying to do what we were told, afraid of making mistakes. However superior you may be in ability, international rugby is eighty per cent confidence.

That defeat really was the last nail for Jonathan. He was captain against Romania and was the focus for most of the criticism of our performance. It came on top of New Zealand and the way his offer to contribute to the committee of inquiry had been refused. I spoke to Jonathan before he left and it was clear he had had enough of the way things were going. Rugby league had been pursuing him for some time and it saw its chance to make the offer he could not refuse.

Jonathan's departure heightened the sense of upheaval. I remember frequent conversations in this period with Bleddyn, Paul Moriarty and John Devereux: 'What is going on here?' 'When is it all going to settle down?' 'When are we going to be allowed to play rugby the right way again?' We should have had a good Five Nations in 1989, building on the success of the year before. Instead, it was a poor year: we lost our first three games against Scotland, Ireland and France. I missed the trip to Murrayfield on 21 January because I went down with pneumonia over Christmas. Jonathan Griffiths played, with Bleddyn as his outside-half. It is always worrying to miss a game. You know that if the person who comes in to replace you plays well, you could lose your place for good. I do not believe anyone who says that they want the person who is playing instead of them to do well. Of course you sit on the bench or in front of the television and you still want Wales to win, and if you are on the bench you say 'all the best' to whoever is playing because that is the done thing. But you really do not want them to do well.

Jonathan had been playing very well, particularly in a televised game against Neath just before Christmas. There had been talk that if he did well against Scotland, this could be his opportunity to be in for a while. It did not happen for him. Edinburgh was always a difficult place to go – we did not win there during my time with Wales – and this was one of those days when you got the ball going backwards, generally with John Jeffrey already standing on your feet. Jonathan was put under a lot of pressure, and did not pass very well. It opened the door for my return, which I did for the matches against Ireland and France.

Wales had never lost all four matches of a Five Nations season, but we were expected to do so when England came to Cardiff on 18 March for the final match of the season. They had had their best season in years – this was the season when the team which dominated the first half of the 1990s came together – and a win would have given them the championship. We beat them 12–9. It was a one-off, founded on pride and character. We were determined not to be whitewashed. Bob Norster, in his last game, took control of the line-out, and we realised early on that if I put the ball behind Rory Underwood, he and Jon Webb would struggle to deal with it, particularly with Ieuan putting them under pressure. Our try, by Mike Hall, came from an English defensive error and I had one of those days when all that kicking practice paid off. It wasn't planned – just a matter of noticing a weakness and playing on it. You can win one-off matches like that on passion and character, but you won't win a Grand Slam or Triple Crown that way.

The pressure we had been under made itself apparent after the post-match dinner when Paul Thorburn, who had been captain, lashed out at Stephen Jones of the *Sunday Times* in his speech. We were all amazed by this – we had a lot of respect for Stephen Jones. That was Thorby's style. If he had something to say, he would say it to your face. But perhaps a captain of Wales needed a little more diplomacy.

I was to find out about that myself come November when John Ryan asked me to lead Wales in the first international of the following season, against our bogey team New Zealand. I was captaining Swansea at the time and we had done well against the touring All Blacks. We lost, but we had become the first club to score three tries against them. Neath had also done well, so there was a certain amount of optimism. I remember taking the call from John Ryan in my home in Trebanos. It was a moment to compare with my first cap, another lifelong ambition fulfilled. I remembered that when I won my first cap nearly four years earlier, David Pickering, the captain, had sent good-luck messages to myself and the other new caps, so one of the first things I did was ring Phil Pugh and Gareth Llewellyn, both of whom were winning their first caps against New Zealand, to congratulate them and wish them luck.

Of course we did not beat the All Blacks – they were still far too good for us – but we played with real passion and were not massacred as we had been in our three previous meetings. We felt reasonably confident going into the 1990 Five Nations. So much for optimism. Seeing off the whitewash in 1989 merely postponed it for a year. Anyone who looks at the statistics of my period as captain – played five, lost five – must conclude that I was one of the worst captains in Welsh history!

We were doing reasonably well against France in the opening match at Cardiff on 20 January until our second row Kevin Moseley was sent off for stamping. We then took a real hammering from England at Twickenham. We had lost matches before in my time playing for Wales, but most of the defeats in the Five Nations had been comparatively narrow, within a score or two. Only New Zealand, and to a lesser extent France in Paris in 1989, had really trounced us. But England absolutely demolished us. We lost 34–6 and were probably lucky it was not more. We did not lose for lack of trying either. They were simply much better than we were – big, powerful and confident. Will Carling, my old adversary, shook me off on the way to running through Mark Titley for England's first try. Mark, a hugely gifted footballer whose form for Swansea had brought him back into the Wales team after a four-year absence, did not play for Wales again.

There is a famous photograph taken in the aftermath of that try, showing Brian Moore saying something which does not appear to be very complimentary to our second row Andy Allen, who is replying with a V-sign. Andy tried as hard as anyone in that match, and had earned his place on the back of his performances for Newbridge. But he was a good example of a Welsh player who came nowhere near his potential. He had everything you need for a top-class player, except dedication. Perhaps if someone had got hold of him at seventeen or eighteen and convinced him how good he could be, he might have stayed on the right road. Instead, he was a typical social rugby player, happier being a local boy enjoying a good social life than a dedicated athlete. Andy was a local club darts champion who was quite capable of downing ten pints and a curry every night. In the professional era he would either have had to knuckle down to the disciplines demanded by a top club or give up top-flight rugby.

In my speech after the dinner I apologised to John Ryan for our performance. We had simply not been good enough as individuals, and once England were completely on top we had rather thrown in the towel. John had felt under pressure even before the England match, and there were rumours that he might resign. At the press conference after the match he clearly did not want to be there, and I ended up taking nearly all the questions. Shortly afterwards he did resign, and we were back to square one, looking for a new coach in the middle of a Five Nations season.

To be fair to the Welsh Rugby Union, this was not the ideal time to be looking for a replacement coach. There was no question of being able to take time to consider options. There was no time, and very little in the way of options. They did the obvious thing: look at the club scene and see who is enjoying the most success. Neath, the cup holders – it was the Schweppes Cup in those days – were on their way to winning it again and would become the first league champions in 1991. Their coach was Ron Waldron, who had played for Wales in the 1960s and as a coach had achieved a lot of success with teams many of whose players were regarded as little more than decent club players. His Neath teams were incredibly fit and committed – Brian Williams, the prop forward who also played occasionally on the flank, was one of the strongest people I have ever met – and had a real 'never say die' spirit. That spirit was instilled by Ron, who had an amazing will to win and was as passionate about rugby and Wales as anybody.

So Ron got the job, and we embarked on yet another complete change of philosophy. There was an understandable influx of Neath players into the squad. Ron had only a short time to get into the job and prepare for the remaining matches in the season, and he naturally enough wanted people around him whom he knew fitted in with his philosophy and played the way he wanted. There were some excellent players among them – Allan Bateman made his international debut in Ron's first match – but not all of them made the necessary leap in standards to the international game.

Ron also introduced to the national set-up the Neath fitness regime. Again, this was what Ron knew and believed in. It had worked well for Neath, producing a team which could run all day every day. But it was a crazy thing to do in the middle of the season. You don't get fit overnight, and training methods based around four-mile runs with heavy fitness sessions in the last few days before an international match were a huge culture shock to players used to different styles of fitness training at their own clubs and previously with Wales. Ron's philosophy was very much 'organised chaos', our strength and stamina wearing down the opposition and forcing them into errors. It had worked very well at club level, but was less successful in internationals.

We lost our remaining two Five Nations matches, against Scotland and Ireland, and by the end I felt shell-shocked. I felt the pressure of being captain and did not feel in full control of the way I was playing. I was used to feeling in control at club and international level and working in a system where players' views and ideas were integral. That had started to unravel when John Ryan came in, and now I felt undermined by everything that was going on around me, even though I was still captain. The end of our season was summed up by a ten-minute spell against Scotland where we were camped on their line and had a succession of scrums. Mark Jones was at number eight and we had several goes at getting across the line, but nothing worked.

That was the end of my time as captain of Wales. I was chosen to lead the tour of Namibia in May and June, but I injured my ankle in the cup semi-final against Neath. Kevin Phillips, who was captaining Neath, took over as captain, and Chris Bridges, also from Neath, whom I knew Ron rated very highly, went as first-choice scrum-half. It gave Chris the chance to establish himself as a serious candidate for the position.

Come the start of the 1991 Five Nations I knew I was under pressure. I was chosen against England on 19 January, although there were reports that Ron had wanted Chris Bridges and had been outvoted. We lost 25–6, our first defeat against them in Cardiff for 28 years – although it was not the worst day in Welsh rugby history as both Neil Jenkins and Scott Gibbs made their debuts – and I went off with a shoulder injury. The injury was partly self-inflicted. I knew Ron was not one hundred per cent convinced that I was the right scrum-half and was determined to show that I could play the physical game he wanted. My adrenalin was flowing and it got me into trouble when Jerry Guscott, a friend from the 1989 Lions tour – although no opponent is a friend when Wales play England – was tackled near the touchline. I went flying in to land on him, and injured my shoulder in the process.

I should not have played in the next match against Scotland, but the trouble is that when you are under pressure for your place you do not want to give your rival a chance. The medical staff put me through a fitness test, but allowed me to make the decision. I said I was fit. I should have been honest with myself and admitted that I was not. I was about 75 per cent, and you cannot play an international in that condition. You are bound to hold back. There are lessons here for players – don't play if you are less than a hundred per cent, as you are bound to be found out – and medical staff: if a player is sent to you for a decision on his fitness you should put him through a rigorous session which will establish whether or not he is OK, whatever he says. We were hammered 32–12 and I was dropped.

I was expecting it, although I was annoyed that nobody explained the decision to me at the time. I said so in the press, the first time I had expressed any real discontent publicly. Ron did ring me a little later, perhaps as a result of that. But the honest truth is that I was almost relieved, things were getting so bad. There had been divisions from the moment Ron was appointed. His co-selectors Geoff Squire and David Burcher seemed to want to have nothing to do with him. At squad sessions they would be on one side of the field while Ron, fitness coach Alan Roper and Dai Richards, who was looking after the backs, were on the other. Geoff and David resigned before very long, but that sort of thing is noticed by players. As the Neath influence grew, so the squad became much more cliquey. People began talking behind others' backs. This was not always the Neath players' fault; if anything, more of the talk was by other small groups behind the backs of Ron and the Neath players (and I have to admit that I was one of those players laughing and joking about some of the ludicrous things that were going on). There were serious undercurrents of animosity floating around the dressing room, steadily growing.

Everyone remembers the way things fell apart on the Australia tour, but the truth is that what happened there was merely the culmination of divisions and frustrations that had built up over the previous eighteen months. We were suffering from a national identity crisis. We weren't Wales any more, united in our desire to do well for our country. That is not to say we did not want to do well, but the divisions were so deep we felt disabled.

On tour, Ron continued to insist on the Neath fitness programme, and this continued to be a problem. During the first week we were in Western Australia. Our training ground was a mile and a half from the hotel. We were told to run there, then the session began with running. At the end, after a full session, we were made to run back. This was not unusual. We would have distance runs perhaps two or three times a week, plus perhaps a session of ten 100-yard sprints. On one occasion as we ran back to the hotel after a session we were passed by Ron who leaned out of his car window and shouted, 'Get a move on, you lazy bastards!' It was ludicrous. There is much more to match fitness than the ability to run. We needed to be fit, but we needed even more to be able to play as a team.

Ron and I soon fell out, over an incident following the game against Australian Capital Territory. I was captain that day, and on the top table at the after-match dinner their captain offered us tickets for a club. On the way back I said to Ron, 'We've got these tickets. Could we stop the bus at the club and allow anyone who wants to to stop off for a while and unwind?' It was the wrong thing to say and do. Ron did not stop us going, but clearly he wasn't happy.

So a group of us went along and had a few drinks. When we got back to the hotel we were certainly merry, but none of us was falling down drunk. We knew we had to get up for training the following morning. The next day, Ron ripped into us all. He said, 'I cannot believe you went out drinking only four days before your next game!' I came in for my share: 'Robert Jones – British Lion, my arse! You were out on the piss last night!' He then made it clear how unhappy he was with much of the squad by saying, 'I am naming this team with bile in my mouth.'

Attitudes towards drink have changed with the introduction of professionalism, and now you can see Ron's point. He could argue that he was simply ahead of his time but, if so, he was too far ahead. This was 1991. We were amateurs going out for a drink, just a couple to relax. It was an accepted part of touring. The 1989 Lions went out regularly together. It was important as a way of bringing us together as a team. Fergus Slattery has told me some extraordinary stories about the sessions the 1971 and 1974 Lions, the most successful teams in our history, used to have.

The following weekend we played New South Wales. We went out feeling as though we had already played a full match. Thorby warmed us up in the dressing room beforehand and it went on for nearly half an hour. My shirt was soaked when we went out, and we were knackered. They were awesome, utterly brilliant; it was one of the best team performances I have ever been on the receiving end of. You would make a tackle, think you had stopped them and find that they were twenty yards further down the field still passing the ball among themselves. David Campese, whom Ron labelled 'a shitty-arsed winger' in his pre-match talk, scored five tries and we lost 71–8. That comment was typical of the bizarre things Ron used to say. On other occasions he had said that he wanted us to play 'like mangy dogs and scalded cats'. By this time we were hanging on his every word, expecting him to foul up at some point. It was wrong, but that was the stage we had reached.

An illustration of how bad things got was this incident at Surfer's Paradise in Queensland. Ron spotted Gareth Llewellyn eating a lollipop and he ripped into him, saying, 'You're a grown man and supposed to be an international rugby player! Your father would be ashamed of you if he could see you!' By this stage, Ron was beginning to feel let down by his squad. He ordered Scott Gibbs to stand up on the table and take his top off. 'That's the sort of thing I'm after!' Ron shouted, pointing at Scott's torso. 'Look at him – he's like a pocket battleship!' Scott looked pretty embarrassed. Ron worked himself up to such a pitch that I thought he was going to hit Gareth.

Afterwards, a group of four or five of us went out for a walk and we came across a shop which was selling these lollipops. We bought up about thirty of them. That evening there was a function with the host union and we all walked in eating these things. It was wrong and childish, and I look back on it with a certain amount of embarrassment, but it showed the way people were feeling at that stage.

By this time Ron had fallen out with Clive Rowlands, who was the manager of the team and was used to being kept informed about selection and to having some say. Ron selected the teams by himself and released them before telling Clive what he had decided, which left Clive very disappointed.

I knew I was unlikely to win selection for the test on 22 July after the débâcle against New South Wales, and as I expected Chris Bridges got the nod. The test was another disaster.

We lost 63–6, but what everybody remembers is the trouble at the after-match banquet. The honest truth is that I did not see exactly what happened. There had been a fair amount of bickering going on among the Welsh lads; bread rolls were being thrown and there was clearly something of an 'us and them' feeling about the night. There had been talk of the rest of the team ganging up on the Neath lads, although I had no part in that. I got on very well with the Neath lads, like Kevin

Phillips, John Davies and Gareth Llewellyn. At some point in the evening Mike Hall cut his hand. Kevin Phillips's name often comes up in connection with this, but I did not see Kevin as a troublemaker. He stuck up for people he knew and respected and he had a great deal of respect for Ron. Whenever we talked about Ron, Kevin would be there arguing his case. He got upset when he felt people were undermining him or not treating him with respect.

When Ron resigned the post not long after the tour had finished, a lot of people thought he had been pushed out. I believe the medical reasons given were genuine. Ron was incredibly intense and passionate about what he was doing, and I can believe the job would have put his health under strain. I disagreed with the way he did things, but I always liked him as a man and respected his commitment. If passion alone were sufficient, he would have been a great national coach. The mistake was to believe that you could build a national team around a single club and its style. It was a lesson the WRU should have learned, but within four years they were to make exactly the same error again.

For now, the WRU yet again found itself looking for a coach at short notice, and with important games coming up – the World Cup was due to take place that autumn. This time they made what I thought was a good choice, bringing in Alan Davies with Gareth Jenkins as his assistant and Bob Norster as manager. Alan came from Ynysybwl but had worked for years in England. He had been coach of Nottingham, making them into one of the best teams in England, and had spent three years in the England set-up as coach of their B side. He brought with him the same advantages we saw several years later with the appointment of Graham Henry: he was an outsider with none of the baggage that anyone connected with the Welsh game would bring with them, and he was bringing objectivity and new ideas to the set-up. It was encouraging to know that Clem Thomas, for whose views I always had a lot of respect, was a great admirer of Alan's abilities as a coach. Gareth Jenkins, too, was a well-respected club coach who had already enjoyed a lot of success with Llanelli. He is one of the nicest people you are likely to meet in rugby as well. Bob had played with many of us – he had only given up the game through injury a couple of years earlier – and was highly respected as a world-class, highly disciplined player.

From the outset the atmosphere was more relaxed. Alan called a meeting with some senior players – Ieuan, Mike Hall, Mike Griffiths, Phil Davies and myself – and indicated that he wanted us to go forward together rather than simply impose his ideas on us. The approach was going to be more structured than it had been under Tony Gray and Derek Quinnell as the game had moved on since 1988, but there would be a return to something like the outlook of the time. Alan came from the English tradition, which was much more forwards- and set-piece-oriented, almost regimented for want of a better word, and he brought some of those disciplines with him. But at the same time he wanted to combine those structures with the best of the Welsh tradition and was always telling us that it was vital we should be ourselves on the field, and not feel shackled. He was very relaxed and approachable personally, as were Gareth and Bob, so an excellent rapport quickly built up between players and coaching staff.

Paul Thorburn had retired from international rugby after the Australian tour, so there was a vacancy for captain as well. There was some speculation that I might get the job again, but they went for Ieuan. It was a good decision, for us and for Ieuan. He has acknowledged how being captain changed his attitude to the game and made him more committed. Up to that point he had tended to live on his talent, which was immense, and at times his weight had nudged the sixteen-stone mark; once he became captain he realised that he had to set an example on and off the field. He became a much more dedicated player and started to get the best out of that talent.

I had felt very low after the Australian tour, for the first time wondering whether international rugby was worth all the trouble and effort we put into it. Alan's appointment restored my enjoyment and confidence. Unfortunately, we had only a limited amount of time to prepare for the World Cup and ran into another disaster, against Western Samoa, in our opening match at Cardiff on 6 October.

The Samoans took us by surprise. We had played them a couple of times before, beating them without too much trouble. We knew they had brought in some decent players like Pat Lam and Peter Fatialofa the piano mover (we always suspected he could move them single-handed), but we knew nothing about people like Frank Bunce. We knew they would tackle ferociously, but were confident that we had the skills to cope with them. We were wrong. Their tackling knocked us completely on to the back foot. Scott Gibbs and Tony Clement in particular took a battering; Tony had a bruise that extended from the top of his leg to his ribcage. They were as hard to play against as the Tongans, but it was all legal and they were much better footballers. We never got into our stride. Even so, I do not believe we would have lost the game had the referee not wrongly awarded them a try almost immediately after half-time. I touched the ball down behind our line, getting my body right over the ball. A Samoan came in straight afterwards and touched down, and the French referee, who was a fair way behind the play, gave the try. I know for a fact that I touched down first, and the television pictures backed me up. It was an absolute killer blow, and it summed up the day for us.

We were always struggling to make the quarter-finals after that 16–13 defeat. We beat Argentina, but then needed to beat Australia at the National Stadium to qualify. They were much too good for us. John Eales and Rod McCall completely dominated the line-out, allowing us to win only three or four all day. The only compensation for the 38–3 loss was that they were an extremely good side and went on to win the cup. After the Australian match we still had the slimmest of hopes – Argentina had to beat Samoa by some unlikely score like 3–0 – but the situation was a pretty forlorn one, and after the first ten minutes of the game we knew we were out, picked up our bags and went home.

In spite of this we felt optimistic going into the 1992 Five Nations. We had had a little longer to get used to Alan and to realise what a perceptive analyst of the game he was. We got used to the fact that if we watched match videos with Alan, he would spot things we did not. You would look again and think, 'Yeah, he's right.' I remember him once talking to me about the options available from a scrum close to the left-hand touchline: 'If you break blind you won't find much space, but you've got the skills to find space somewhere else. If you break open where the backlines are, the chances are that their right-winger will follow across to cover the move. That will leave space behind him. If you run just a yard or two open and kick back into the left-hand box so that the ball will roll and your left-winger is aware that you might do this, he could get a ten- to fifteen-yard start.' We never had a move like that in our repertoire, but the idea was typical of Alan's ability to spot little things and his desire to work with individuals, using their skills and improving their vision. Most importantly, he was not telling you that you had to play this way, it was more a question of making us more aware of the possibilities. He emphasised that any moves we practised were merely options and that it was important we retain our initiative.

Our sense of optimism looked to be justified by the win in Ireland on 18 January. Stuart Davies, who had been my opponent at the ages of eleven and thirteen and my team-mate since fifteen, won his first cap and scored the winning try. We had another new outside-half in Colin Stephens from Llanelli, with Neil Jenkins moving to play alongside Scott Gibbs at centre. Colin was a typical Welsh outside-half. He was very quick, a good kicker and an excellent all-round ball-player. He was a very quick bowler in cricket, too. I had seen him playing in a Schools international at St Helen's only two or three years earlier, and he'd scored a superb try from halfway with three side-steps and sheer pace. The general reaction had been 'it's Jonathan Davies all over again'. He looked a superb player at club level and started well for Wales, but he never fulfilled his promise. The one thing he really lacked was confidence. This was his only season in the Wales side and he was devastated when he was dropped after the third game of the campaign, against England (I suspect his views on Alan Davies might not be as positive as mine). I remember meeting him shortly afterwards and him saying, 'I know I'm good enough, if only I get another chance.'

Beating Ireland was important because we had not won a Five Nations match for two seasons. It was a huge relief. BBC Wales ran a trailer campaign using 'The Boys are Back in Town' as its theme tune for our next game against France, on 1 February. We came closer than we usually did to beating them, going down 12–9, and were then well beaten by England at Twickenham. At least we finished with a win against Scotland. Two wins out of four might not seem a great record, but it certainly felt like progress after only one win and a draw in the previous three seasons, and we felt we were heading in the right direction.

The following year started well too. We beat England at Cardiff in February, thanks to a moment of opportunism by Ieuan and some poor play by them. I can't to this day work out what Rory Underwood was doing – anyone would think the hotel had spiked his Coke (Rory does not drink alcohol) – but he dawdled back after a kick ahead by Emyr Lewis and Ieuan came from a long way back to overtake him and score. It was largely down to the doziness of the English defence, but Ieuan still had to spot the opportunity and take it.

This 10–9 win over the double Grand Slam champions produced another real surge of optimism and we took a huge following to Murrayfield later in the month. But the pattern throughout my career had been that odd-numbered years were tough. We had to play Scotland at Murrayfield, where we never won, Ireland at Cardiff – a game which for some reason we almost always lost, although we usually beat them in Dublin – and France in Paris – and we couldn't beat them anywhere. The one game we were likely to win going by past performances – indeed, the only one we did, in 1987, 1989 and 1993 – was England in Cardiff. The same pattern was followed in 1993. We were absolutely hammered, 20–0, at Murrayfield and then had another nightmare against Ireland at Cardiff. I was dropped for the final match, against France in Paris, and did not get back into the side for more than a season.

Alan explained to me that the forwards were not delivering enough good ball to make the best use of my strengths, and he felt that Rupert Moon's more physical style was better suited to the poor ball we were getting. I did not agree with him – the irony was that at the time I was playing my best club rugby in a long time – but at least Alan did it the right way, taking the trouble to explain the decision to me and making it clear that I still had a role to play. If that approach had been adopted more generally during my career, not just with me but with others like Bleddyn Bowen, we might have made rather more of the talent available to us.

I also thought that Rupert should not have been selected on the simple grounds that he is not Welsh. You can say, as many people have done, that he has spent a long time in Wales and has become one of us. But to my mind he had pledged himself to England by playing for a whole series of their representative sides: colts, students, all the way up to England A. He was playing for England Students against England in one of their World Cup warm-up matches only a few months before he decided he wanted to play for Wales. A national identity is not something you can change over-night. Having Rupert play scrum-half for Wales, with Dewi Morris opposite him in an England shirt, did not make a great deal of sense to me.

I thought Rupert was an extremely good club player and he did a decent job for Wales – after all, we won the champion-ship with him at scrum-half in 1994, and you can't argue with that – but it is always frustrating watching somebody you think is not as good a player as you, and who you do not believe should be qualified to play. We did not get on badly, although I did find Rupert, being such a showman, a little hard to take at times. He seemed to turn up with a different hat for every meal, although he has obviously settled on a beret in recent years. We started to get to know each other a little better after a while and have got on very well since we finished playing international rugby – at least I thought Rupert had finished playing international rugby, and I suspect he did as well until he was suddenly recalled in 2000 – and Rupert was a great help when I had my testimonial, going out of his way to promote it on his radio show. I was sorry that I could not return the compliment when he had his testimonial. I was asked to play, but at the time I was on holiday with my family.

As a scrum-half you are very dependent on the quality of possession you get from your forwards. I spent a lot of my Wales career receiving the ball going backwards, either from the scrum or loose taps off the top of the line-out. Our scrum was rarely secure, and Welsh packs over the years have had a tendency to deliver the ball in a rather cumbersome manner: the ball would simply be put in and would work its way to the number eight, who might hold it for a while. I also spent a lot of my time digging for the ball at rucks and mauls, something scrum-halves are generally spared under the current rules. Over the years, we have not been as organised up front as we might have been. Having said all I have about the importance of players having a variety of skills, you still need some basic organisation, and this applies to the front five more than any other part of the team. At times I think our forwards were rather too keen to get the ball in hand, and not sufficiently focused on the basic tasks of ball-winning. That has to be got right, or everything else becomes next to impossible.

I probably should have been more assertive with my forwards rather than accepting the rubbish that was often shovelled back at me. People used to say to me, 'Rob, if they do that, just kick it back at them.' But I could not do that.

After all, I knew that they weren't trying to give me bad ball. But perhaps I should have handed out a good rollicking. I suspect that one or two of our forwards did think, 'Don't worry, Rob'll cope with it.' Rupert probably looked more assertive. He was certainly always talking to the forwards.

The frustrating thing from my point of view was that almost as soon as I was left out, the forwards started delivering decent ball. In 1994, we had a decent scrummage, with Ricky Evans and John Davies providing real stability. Scott Quinnell made a big impact in his first season at number eight, and Emyr Lewis, who was a superb forward when he was in the right mood, had one of his good years. Phil Davies also forced his way back into the team. Players go through phases in their careers, and Phil clearly had a fresh burst of enthusiasm and confidence that year. He had always been a talented player, and he flourished when the people around him were good enough to make use of those talents.

It was frustrating watching that championship-winning Five Nations campaign from the bench, although I did get on for a few rather alarming minutes in the win over Ireland in Dublin on 5 February. Nigel Davies was hurt and we had already had several injuries, so I wound up on the wing with three or four minutes to go and Wales leading by only a couple of points. I did not get a touch. More importantly, nor did Simon Geoghegan, who was playing opposite me and might have fancied his chances against a makeshift winger. I was also given a run-out that May in the World Cup qualifying match against Portugal in Lisbon – not the most demanding game of rugby I have played in. We won 102–11. I even scored a couple of tries. In 2000, I made sure the tries I scored against England in 1987 and Scotland in 1995 made it into the *101 Great Welsh Tries* video I helped put together; had I been able to lay hands on any film of this game against Portugal, those ones would have gone in as well!

Alan had always made it clear that my exclusion from the side was a consequence of our problems up front rather than an outright judgement on the way I was playing, and he soon showed that, as usual, he was as good as his word. A lot of people said I was in with a chance after captaining the Barbarians against the Springboks in Dublin in December 1994. The game went very well and we beat them, which was particularly enjoyable because they had slaughtered the All Whites at St Helen's. Gareth Jenkins made the call which told me I was back in for the game against France at the beginning of the 1995 Five Nations.

I had a few good moments personally. While I was normally not terribly concerned about personal records, getting my fiftieth cap in the England match at Cardiff on 18 February was something special. I was only the third Welshman to achieve this feat, following Gareth Edwards and J.P.R. Williams – not bad company to be in. Running out at the head of the team on an occasion like that is something you never forget, as I am sure Gareth Thomas, who achieved his fiftieth in Italy in 2001, and Rob Howley, who will surely get his in the first international of the 2001/2 season, would confirm. I also scored a try in the first few minutes of the match against Scotland at Murrayfield on 4 March, and I thought it was one of my best games for Wales – and not just because I scored.

But nothing could disguise the fact that it was another terribly disappointing year. After winning the championship in 1994, we were whitewashed. Perhaps the other teams were a little more wary of us after the previous season. We had certainly run out of luck. Scott Quinnell had gone to rugby league before the season started, and there was another blow to our pack in the first few minutes of the first game when Ricky Evans was butted by Olivier Merle, the French lock, and his ankle broke as he fell to the floor. Ricky had done superbly the previous year, but managed only nine minutes of the 1995 championship. John Davies was sent off against England, Phil's form dipped (he would be left out of the World Cup squad) and Emyr Lewis was not the force he had been in 1994. Given all this, it was not very surprising that we reverted to struggling up front.

We were soon under pressure. By this stage, the crowd at Cardiff was very quick to get on our backs when things went wrong. It was not that you heard anything specific, but it was not hard to catch the mood, and a sour one was undoubtedly inhibiting to a struggling team. Indeed, it was becoming easier to play away from home because of the pressure. Alan Davies was under more of it than anyone. I still had no doubt that he was the right man for the job, and said so after the Scotland game when he was starting to receive heavy criticism in the papers. The players respected him, Bob and Gareth, and were looking forward to them taking us to the World Cup in South Africa in May. It was our fault, not theirs, that we were not performing. But by this stage there were clearly backstage machinations, people within the Welsh Rugby Union who wanted them out. Alan would say quite openly to the players that he was not getting support from the union. He'd joke about it, saying, 'I've just been to a meeting with the WRU committee. Someone take the knives out of my back, please.' He resigned at the end of March, along with Bob and Gareth, a few days after we lost the final match at home to Ireland. It was described as a resignation, but my strong impression was that Alan and his team had been pushed into a corner and felt they had little option. It was a terrible piece of timing, with only two months to go before the World Cup.

Once again the WRU had to find a coach at short notice, and went for the most successful club coach. Alec Evans had done well with Cardiff, and because he was an Australian he was seen as an outsider, with the advantages that confers. By this stage there was also an exaggerated respect for anyone with a southern hemisphere accent. It was assumed that they must be better than anybody who had come through the Welsh system.

At the time I thought it was probably the right decision in the circumstances. It turned out to be a serious mistake. Alec brought a lot of baggage with him, and for the second time we endured an attempt to remake Wales in the image of a single club. As for Ron Waldron, you can make a case for what he did. When you have to take a team over at such short notice and take it to the World Cup, it is natural to decide that you want around you the people you know and trust. Ieuan had been captain for the last three and a half years and we expected him to lead us in the World Cup, but Alec chose Cardiff's Mike Hall as his captain. Mike is intelligent, articulate and very confident, and he did a decent job in difficult circumstances.

During part of the World Cup I was rooming with Andy Moore from Cardiff, who had been chosen as the other scrum-half. Alec used to ring him up and talk to him for twenty to thirty minutes at a time every day. He did the same with other Cardiff players, like Derwyn Jones and Hemi Taylor. They used to meet in his room and go for meals together. Now, you just can't do that sort of thing as a coach who has come from a club side into a national set-up. You need to integrate everyone in the squad, not have a small group who are your players and exclude the rest. Alec had had a great deal of success with Cardiff, and their players had a great respect for him, but the rest of us were subjected to yet another change of tactics – if you can dignify what went on in South Africa with the word. The strategy was to win possession and then kick the ball as far as we could down the field. The idea was that the other team would kick badly or make some other mistake. That really was just about it.

During one of our training sessions in Johannesburg the ball was kicked to Tony Clement who decided on his own initiative to run it back. He had gone about fifteen yards when Alec blew his whistle and said, 'You don't do that. You don't run the ball back. We're at altitude. You kick it back.' That attitude was drummed into us. It did not work. In our final match against Ireland on 4 June we kicked everything long and it clearly was not working; Ireland were kicking better and further than we were, and we were continuously driven back. I said to Mike Hall, 'We can't go on doing this. This is getting us nowhere.' Mike simply said, 'We've got to carry on.' We played some half-decent rugby in the last fifteen minutes, more out of desperation than anything, but Ireland held on to beat us 24–23 and we could not complain. We did not deserve to win after playing like that. It was a lousy way to finish my international career – although I did not know at the time it was the end.

The really annoying thing about the whole experience was that Alec refused to accept any responsibility for our performance. He said afterwards, 'I can only coach them off the field. Then it is up to them.' The truth was that for 65 minutes we had played in the style he had forced on us and were outplayed. He said he had not coached us to play that way, but in fact he coached us incessantly. He was not up to the job and was found out quickly at the World Cup, but we would still have felt some respect for him had he been prepared to shoulder some of the responsibility.

When we got back to Wales, Alec gave an interview alleging that a group of us had been out on the piss just before one of the games. The only person he named was Mike Ruddock, but he also talked about 'senior players' and was clearly aiming at people like Stuart Davies, Tony Clement and myself. About three weeks before the World Cup, Alec had imposed a complete alcohol ban on the squad. And it is true that a group, probably about fifteen or sixteen of us, went out for a couple of beers – no more – several days before one of the games. There does come a time when you need to relax and get away from the hotel and training sessions for a short while; it was not as if there was much to do in Bloemfontein anyway. It was a chance to relax and get together as a group, something we badly needed to do to build some spirit in the team. Alec turned a couple of drinks a few days before a game into an all-night piss-up.

It just wasn't the truth. Nobody in that team would have been that irresponsible. We were in South Africa to play in the greatest rugby tournament in the world. I was incensed when I read his comments. I had always taken care of myself and made sure that rugby came first. I had made sure that I rested properly, ate sensibly before matches and did not over-exert myself on the day before matches – for instance ensuring that I never drove very far, as a long time in the car can leave you tired and stiff. Everything was geared to making sure I was in the best possible shape for the match. But I felt that Alec was bent on blaming everybody but himself for the fact that we had played badly.

He had fallen out with Mike Ruddock at an early stage on that trip, mainly over team selection. When the team was announced for the opening match against Japan, Andy Moore was chosen. Of course I was disappointed because I wanted to play, but Alec said to me, 'Don't worry, I'm keeping you for the important matches against New Zealand and Ireland.' A little later I bumped into Mike in the corridor of the hotel. He said, 'Are you happy?' 'Fine,' I replied. 'Alec has tipped me the wink that I'll be in against New Zealand and Ireland.' 'I wouldn't believe a word he tells you,' Mike came back. 'I had one hell of a struggle to get you on this trip at all. There was a lobby for bringing Andy Moore and Paul John.'

To be fair, Alec did pick me against New Zealand and Ireland, but at the start of the 1995/6 season Wales went back to South Africa on a short tour and, despite the fact that I was playing in South Africa for Western Province at the time, nobody asked me about my availability. The first squad of the domestic season, for the match against Fiji on 11 November, was announced at the end of September. Andy Moore, Paul John and Rob Howley were the scrum-halves. I was not in, for the first time in ten seasons. I did not find out from anyone in the Welsh Rugby Union, but from a reporter who rang me for a comment. I was absolutely gutted that nobody had had the decency to tell me I was being left out or to give me an explanation why.

A couple of days later I was at a boxing night at Cardiff Rugby Club – it was the night Steve Robinson fought Naseem Hamed. I bumped into Peter Thomas, the chairman of Cardiff, who said to me, 'Alec wants you to know that he is gutted you were not included. He wants you to know he had nothing to do with it, that he was outvoted.' My reaction was along the lines of: 'He's the coach, for God's sake. Is he telling me he has no influence on selection?' Soon after that I bumped into Derek Quinnell, who was one of the selectors. He told me that Alec had come into the meeting with the list of players he wanted chosen and had been given what he wanted. Somebody was clearly not telling the truth, and Derek Quinnell and Mike Ruddock are both people I have known for years. I respect them enormously and would trust them as completely as I would members of my family.

The poison that I believe was spilled by Alec, and one or two other people such as Hemi Taylor, stayed in Welsh rugby for a while. It even cost Swansea a match against Cardiff the following season. Stuart Davies was hardly mates with Hemi at the best of times, and for once he forgot to play his own game and allowed himself to be caught up in his feelings. We followed his example.

I always had a regard for the basic integrity of John Ryan and Ron Waldron, even when I disagreed with what they were doing as coaches. There was never any doubt about their desire to succeed for Wales. In my opinion, Alec failed hopelessly as a coach, then tried to shift all the blame on to his players. He did the damage, then made his escape, resigning before the Fiji game was played.

I was not included in Kevin Bowring's first squad. I had no problem with not being warned about that because I had no history with Kevin and he had no obligation to me. But I did speak to him to check that I had not been excluded because of anything Alec might have said. Kevin, another decent, honourable man, explained that it was his decision and he was not going to select players who would not be around for the next World Cup in 1999. I said that I expected I would still be around then, but I was happy to have been given an honest answer.

Kitch Christie, who won the World Cup for South Africa in 1995, has argued that your aim must be to pick a side that can win its next game. If you spend your time thinking three or four years ahead you can lose sight of the present, lose matches and drain confidence so that the development you hope for never takes place. Clive Woodward has also said that he made the mistake of trying to think three years ahead when he got the England job, and that he did not intend to make the same error twice. But we have to accept that the four-year World Cup cycle is a fact of life, dominating everything else in rugby. In the autumn of 1995 I was on the scrapheap, discarded and not yet thirty. I was not the only one either. Tony Clement, a year younger than me, also won his last cap against Ireland, and it took Stuart Davies a couple of years to get back into the side.

It was disappointing to finish like that, particularly when you consider the high hopes Wales had at the beginning of my international career and the way it had looked in the late 1980s, as though many of those hopes would be fulfilled. We had fallen back, lurching from coach to coach and style to style, while other countries raced ahead. I started my international career playing in a team encouraged to think for itself and to express its talents and vision; I finished in one that had been told the only way to play was to kick the ball as far forward as possible, and had failed even to do that very well. Wales is still recovering from the mistakes of those years.

My country's fortunes on and off the field of play may have been in the doldrums, but it was a while yet before I was prepared to accept that my international career was over.

# 9 King Henry?

'The idea was to have an event in the Grand Theatre in Swansea on the past, present and future of Welsh rugby with a panel comprising myself, Ieuan, Graham Henry and J.P.R. Williams, with Nigel Walker as master of ceremonies. Dan Minster and Dawn Jobbins, who were on the benefit committee, asked me to help them get in contact with Nigel Walker and Graham Henry. I spoke to Nigel and asked him what his fee was; he replied, "Just cover my way. I'll be happy to do it." I then managed to get a number for Graham Henry, and Dan rang him. Henry said he, too, would be happy to do it, but that his fee was £1,500. By the time the event came round, this had risen to around £2,000.'

I T WAS IRONIC that my hopes of playing for Wales again came to an end in 1995 under the new coach Kevin Bowring. Unlike Ieuan and several other leading players, I never formally retired from playing international rugby. I was available until the end of my last season as a senior player. However unlikely it may have become, it did no harm to set myself goals. Indeed, it helped focus and motivate me for each club season. Allan Bateman, who is eight months older than me, takes the same approach. Of course, unlike Allan, after a while I stopped believing that I might get back into the team, but I imagine Rupert Moon did as well before he was recalled in 2000 after six years out!

The irony was that I liked Kevin's approach to coaching Wales. My impression was that he believed in many of the same ideas I have been putting forward in this book. He took the view that there was a distinctive Welsh style of play and he wanted his team to express the best of that approach to the game, players with the freedom and vision to take on opponents using their skills and imagination. He believed we could be successful again playing that way, and for a while his teams looked as though they could repay that belief. He put his faith in players like Arwel Thomas, and when his teams were at their best they were terrific to watch.

The moment that best summed up this new sense of freedom came at Twickenham on 3 February 1996 when we won a kickable penalty in the first few minutes. Everybody expected it to be kicked for three points. England certainly did, and they headed for their own line. Arwel saw what was going on and took a quick tap penalty; some quick hands by Gwyn Jones and Leigh Davies later, Hemi Taylor went over for the try. The really important thing about that moment wasn't that the try was scored, although that was very welcome, it was that Arwel had the confidence and imagination in the first few minutes of his first Five Nations match to try something unexpected. That was typical of Arwel at his best, but it also reflected Kevin Bowring's style. Kevin's teams played with a real sense of imagination and purpose. It was great to watch, and they managed some good results, too: they scared England and France on their own grounds in 1996 and had that terrific win at Murrayfield in January 1997. I really felt that we were starting to progress in the right direction.

An important part of that progression was the development of Robert Howley at scrum-half. Rob was one of those players who emerged from Schools rugby as someone who looked capable of going very quickly into the international game. As soon as you saw him as a youngster at Bridgend, you knew he was going to be an exceptional player. But it took him longer than expected to make the breakthrough and he was not capped until he was 25. Maybe he was not helped by being at Bridgend, not one of the strongest clubs, and his first move to Cardiff did not work out for him. He went on the tour to Canada and the Pacific in 1994 as back-up to Rupert Moon (I was excused to play for Western Province in South Africa), but did not make much of an impact. After that he dropped behind Andy Moore, who went to the 1995 World Cup and played at the start of the 1995/6 season, including the match against Italy on 16 January 1996, which was Kevin's first full game in charge.

Kevin gave Rob his chance in that match against England at Twickenham. I did not know Rob that well, but we had the influence of Geoff Davies – who had coached him at Bridgend – in common and I had always rated him as a player. Before the game I sent him a message wishing him luck. Rob had a great day. He scored a try and played brilliantly. I was watching along with Phil Davies in an S4C hospitality box and have to admit that it was tough to watch. At the time, I was still desperate to return to the Wales team and I knew that with Rob playing so well on debut it would be very hard to get back. Apart from Rob playing well, there were other candidates around as well: Andy Moore was still in contention, along with Paul John. Previously it had tended to be me and one other person, so I was always at least on the bench; now I knew it would be that much more difficult, that perhaps I never would play for my country again.

The disappointing thing was that Wales did not move forward from that promising start under Kevin Bowring. We suffered two massive defeats during the 1998 Five Nations – 60–26 at Twickenham in February and 51–0 to the French at Wembley in April – and at the end of the season Kevin resigned. I still think he had the right ideas and aims, but we went backwards rather than forward. Perhaps Kevin, who is a hell of a nice guy, fell into a bit of a trap that way and was reluctant to take decisions that might upset people, so players got into a bit of a comfort zone. He could probably have done with someone a little more hard-nosed alongside him, although there were not that many obvious candidates around. He was always under pressure, the media calling for his head even more publicly than they had demanded Alan Davies's, and, as with Alan, I wonder if Kevin ever received the support he truly deserved from the union.

After this latest resignation, the WRU announced its intention over the close season to scour the world for the best possible coach and to pay whatever it took to persuade him to take the job. Eventually, Graham Henry was appointed at a reported £250,000 per year – about five times what his predecessor had been on. Only the story was not quite that simple. Before the announcement was made that Henry was the new coach of Wales, Mike Ruddock had been offered and had accepted the post.

Terry Cobner had been to Dublin to meet Mike and, on behalf of the WRU, offer him the job of Wales coach.

Subsequent to that, Mike's solicitor went over to Wales, at Mike's expense, to sort out the details of his contract. Mike had already obtained his release from his previous employers in Leinster and had done an interview with John Kennedy of Westgate, the agency which does the WRU's press and publicity. Then, on the eve of the announcement, he had another call from Kennedy who told him that things were on hold; there was some uncertainty about Ruddock's appointment. The next thing that happened was that Graham Henry was announced as the new coach of Wales. Mike was naturally disappointed and had every right to feel ill-treated, but he is not the sort of man to shout about something like this. He still hopes that one day he will get the chance to coach Wales.

In my opinion, Mike would have been an excellent appointment. He thinks deeply about the game and is a great man-manager who can organise and motivate players, but at the same time gives them the freedom to play. For a former back-row forward, he has a remarkable understanding of the way backs see the game. He did a great job at Swansea and knew the Welsh scene and the available players very well; he had also been away and enjoyed success in Ireland, which broadened his outlook and experience. His record at Swansea would have been enough to give him credibility in Wales, and the time he had spent away would mean that he was not too closely associated with the club. In any case, he is far too intelligent a coach to repeat the error of trying to build a national team around a single club. He would have cost about a third of what was offered to Graham Henry.

I was of course happy that the WRU was trying to get the best coach in the world. So much the better if he turned out to be Welsh, but we were past the point where it was worth being dogmatic about this. Whoever it was was never going to come cheap. But £250,000 a year seemed an awful lot of money for a man with no track record at all in international rugby. He had certainly enjoyed a lot of success with Auckland, but you could look at the quality of the players in that team and legitimately ask how much coaching he actually needed to do to make them successful. And by being so obviously desperate, the WRU made it easy for him to ask for this extraordinary amount of money.

I was not convinced he was the right choice, but he came in and made an immediate impact, not just on the team but on the whole of Wales. He talked a huge amount of sense and was completely honest in his appraisal of the job he had to do. He said it would be a difficult and long-drawn-out task, that there was no sense in expecting miracles. The attitude in Wales was very favourable to him. We had brought in a New Zealander, an outsider with new ideas and no baggage, and given him a five-year contract, and everybody was ready to think long-term and not expect results immediately.

He came in with one other huge advantage: the 96–13 hammering taken by our touring team in South Africa in June 1998. Everybody remembered that result, and our progress afterwards was measured against it. What was forgotten was that the team Wales fielded that day was barely even a second fifteen. The tour should never have taken place. Most of the leading players had refused to go and there were injuries on the tour. I believe that if a South African second or third fifteen came to Wales, we would give them a good hammering.

With this sort of scoreline as the standard, Henry enjoyed almost immediate success, and the people and the media of Wales put him on a pedestal. Within a few months he was probably the most famous person in the country. My father-in-law Clive Rowlands said at the time that if Graham Henry and Gareth Edwards were walking down opposite sides of a street, people would be crossing the road to get Henry's autograph. Henry did not ask for this to happen. He clearly could not believe how much importance people in Wales place on having a successful rugby team. But that is what Wales is like. We invest so much emotion in our team that the mood of the nation changes according to the success or failure of the team.

We had some terrific wins, for which Graham Henry deserves a great deal of credit. Some of the attacking play in the victory in Paris on 6 March 1999 was terrific, although Scotland were to do even better against France a few weeks later. Then there was that win over England at Wembley on 11 April. We were almost completely outplayed for 79 of the 80 minutes, but won for two reasons: Neil Jenkins, as he has been doing for most of his career, was keeping us in the game with his boot; and the players' spirit. Everyone refused to quit and kept on battling until we had our one chance to win, which Scott Gibbs and Neil took. That spirit was something that had perhaps been lacking towards the end of Kevin Bowring's period in charge.

The tour of Argentina that summer was a real test of that character. Battling back to win twice against tough opponents was proof of the sense of self-belief in the team, and again you have to credit Henry for that. And although the win over South Africa on 26 June, with the Millennium Stadium still largely a building site, was not against their strongest possible team, it was still the first time we had beaten the Springboks in thirteen attempts. They certainly were not a bad side or a pushover, and that psychological barrier of beating them still had to be overcome.

We were so delighted to be winning again after years of defeats that there was a real sense of euphoria about the nation. It was still there going into the World Cup that autumn. I was caught up in it myself. At a lunch before the first game against Argentina on 1 October I was asked to say grace. I went through the routine of thanking God for the food we were about to eat and finished with the words, 'And most of all, Lord, we thank you for Graham Henry.' It was intended as a joke. I knew people would laugh, and they did. That was the mood of the nation for the first twelve months of Graham Henry as coach.

We did not do as well as we had hoped in the World Cup, losing to Western Samoa and Australia, although perhaps as well as we could realistically have expected. Going into the new millennium, we began to look at things with a slightly greater sense of proportion, to take a longer look and ask how far we had really come. At the same time I was starting to do more work for radio and for newspapers, which meant I was looking at games more analytically rather than as a player or a fan. It was clear to me by this time that there were a few cracks in the structure.

There were also one or two areas concerning Henry's conduct where I felt some personal concern. I felt, for instance, that he had a tendency to take advantage of his high profile. A good example of that occurred during Paul Arnold's testimonial year with the All Whites. The idea was to have an event in the Grand Theatre in Swansea on the past, present and future of Welsh rugby with a panel comprising myself, Ieuan, Graham Henry and J.P.R. Williams, with Nigel Walker as master of ceremonies. Dan Minster and Dawn Jobbins, who were on the benefit committee, asked me to help them get in contact with Nigel Walker and Graham Henry. I spoke to Nigel and asked him what his fee was; he replied, 'Just cover my way. I'll be happy to do it.' I then managed to get a number for Graham Henry, and Dan rang him. Henry said he, too, would be happy to do it, but that his fee was £1,500. By the time the event came round, this had risen to around £2,000.

It went very well on the night – J.P.R. had to drop out, but his place was ably taken by Mark Davies, the Wales physio and former All Whites and Wales flanker – and there were around 800 people in the Grand. Henry probably added about 500 to the audience, but he also probably made about twice as much out of the evening as Paul Arnold. I must admit that I was sitting on the panel that evening thinking, 'He's already making £250,000 a year. I don't think this is right.' Someone with Graham Henry's knowledge of rugby and eye for detail had to know who Paul Arnold was – he was still playing senior rugby for Swansea and had been in the Wales squad only two or three years earlier – that he was someone who was never going to enjoy many of the benefits of the professional game, in spite of years at the top as an amateur. I still cannot believe that Henry charged him for his appearance.

If I am asked to do something like an after-dinner speech which requires special preparations, then I charge, although I don't like doing it. I have never charged a Welsh rugby club a penny for doing presentations or anything like that. I felt that taking part in a panel session talking about the state of Welsh rugby was in any case part of Graham Henry's job as national coach. Stories about him charging for events were common around this time. More recently, though, I have started meeting people who tell me he is doing their club event for nothing – Betws and Llandybie come to mind – so he has obviously changed his approach.

On a more personal level, I was unhappy about the complete absence of reaction by the Wales set-up when my brother Rhodri was seriously injured in a car crash in the summer of 1999. It was no secret – the reports were in all the papers. Rhodri must have had a letter, a card or a phone call asking how he was and wishing him well from just about every club or invitation team he had ever played for or against, but there was nothing from the WRU or anyone involved in the national set-up. And this, remember, was just after he had been on the Wales tour of Argentina and was in the preliminary squad for the World Cup. Every day I passed on messages to him – there were an unbelievable number of them – and Rhod would say, 'Anything from the WRU?'

I know coaches are under immense pressure, but it should have been the easiest thing in the world for Graham Henry to pick up the phone and ask Rhod, 'How are you?' It would have made a world of difference to him, but to this day it has not happened. Being a coach is not just about on-field organisation, but about dealing with people. That Henry, David Pickering or anyone else in the Wales set-up couldn't even take the slightest interest in a member of their squad who had seen his ambition to play for his country destroyed in an accident was, I feel, a disgrace.

I was also unhappy, long before it was clear that there were problems about qualifications, with the practice of importing players who are not Welsh to play for Wales. There is a simple point of principle here: I believe it is wrong. Where you come from, who your parents are, where your roots are, where you were born – these things should mean everything. Instead, they seem to count for very little. People will always point out that Gwyn Nicholls, who captained the first Wales team to beat the All Blacks in 1905, and one or two other members of that team were born in England and will argue that this has always happened. But Nicholls and the others regarded themselves as Welsh and had made a commitment. A good, more modern example of this was Stuart Barnes, who played Wales Schools rugby and was soon called up to the senior squad. Stuart has a very Welsh attitude to the game and could have had a terrific international career with us, but his view was, 'How can I possibly play for Wales when, whenever there is an international on television, I am cheering for England?' Jon Callard was another who played for Wales Schools (with me), knew he was English and so ended up playing for Bath and England.

I simply can't believe Shane Howarth when he says he regards himself as Welsh. Shane made his commitment when he pulled on the black jersey of New Zealand, just as Rupert Moon did when he played for England A. And then there's Jason Jones-Hughes. Maybe he has got a Welsh father, but he grew up in Australia, played for the Australian Barbarians, which is the nearest thing they have to an A side, and was contracted to the Australian Rugby Union. The Australians were in no great position to complain given their record of poaching players from other countries, but the point is that nobody should be doing this. Peter Rogers, who has Welsh parents and had lived in Wales before going out to South Africa, was a different case, and I had no problem with him being selected.

We certainly cannot complain about the way the likes of Shane Howarth and Brett Sinkinson played before their registrations were exposed as inaccurate. They made out-standing contributions. But I would question how much better they really made Wales. Howarth probably did make a difference – he played extremely well in a position where we have struggled recently. Sinkinson also played well, but he was in direct competition for a place with Martyn Williams, and kept him out of the side. Martyn is one of those players who seems to improve every time he plays for Wales; when he finally got a full season in the team he played well enough to win a place, in one of the more competitive positions, in the 2001 Lions squad to Australia. How much further might he have developed had he been in the side during the period when we were picking Sinkinson?

Bringing in players from the outside instead of developing our own is short-term thinking. Even if it improves the team initially, does it really help us in the longer run? Some of our imports have failed even to help in the short-term. I have nothing against Jason Jones-Hughes, whom I don't know personally, but I cannot see why resources and energy were devoted to recruiting him. Centre is one of the positions in which we have the greatest depth of talent: as well as Scott Gibbs and Mark Taylor, who have played most of the internationals during Graham Henry's reign as coach, we also have players like Allan Bateman, Neil Boobyer, Leigh Davies and the up-and-coming Matthew J. Watkins. The acquisition of Jones-Hughes sent completely the wrong message to someone like Leigh Davies. Leigh should be encouraged to think, 'If I play well enough, I'll have a chance of getting back into the Wales side'; instead, he finds that someone who probably cannot match his abilities and talent is brought in from outside and given the chance that should be his.

Leigh provides a good example of the way we sometimes fail to make the most of the talent we have. He made a superb start when he came into the Wales team as a youngster. Had there been a Lions team in 1996 he would have been selected, and would probably have made the test team. Then he moved to Cardiff, did not develop, and lost his place. He was a terrific young player who should have been encouraged to play his own way and express those excellent natural skills of his. People tend to think of him as a big guy who runs at people, but I know from playing with Leigh at Cardiff when he started performing again to something like his level of talent that his greatest asset is his vision and a great pair of hands. He is very good at creating space for other people. Perhaps it was all a little too easy for him at the start, and of course Scott Gibbs reappearing on the Welsh rugby union scene did not help him. But he should have been encouraged rather than excluded. Leigh is exactly the sort of player who might have benefited from an effective mentoring system, the sort of player who should now be scooped up by development manager Nigel Walker. I can't help thinking that had Leigh emerged in Australia with his range of talents he would have been on his way to sixty or seventy caps rather than being discarded. He was in the 1999 World Cup squad but did not get a game – Jones-Hughes went on as a replacement against Argentina when Scott Gibbs went off.

While the decision to bring Jones-Hughes across raised some doubts about Graham Henry, Wales's performances in that World Cup raised rather more. This was particularly true of the defeat by Samoa. It was striking to hear Pat Lam and Va'aiga Tuigamala saying afterwards that they knew what to expect from Wales because they knew about Henry's approach to rugby from their time in Auckland. They are both exceptional players, and Samoa played extremely well, but when a country that is still trying to establish itself as a leading rugby nation knows exactly what to expect from your coach, and how to counteract it, you have a problem.

The defeat by Australia was also worrying. It was not that we lost – Australia were the best team in the competition and we never had a realistic chance of beating them. The truth is that we gave them a harder game than anyone could have expected, and again you have to give Graham Henry some credit for that. His teams have always been organised and have always played with real commitment. But those are only

starting-points in international rugby. You need some imagination and the ability to do the unexpected as well, and these
qualities were entirely lacking in our play. We did not make
a break all afternoon and were back to relying on Neil
Jenkins to keep us in the game. Nor were there any real
options on the bench for changing the way the game was
being played.

Two years on I feel these problems have still not been fully
addressed. We are solid and well-organised in the set-pieces,
so Robert Howley has generally not had to cope with some of
the difficulties I faced during the early 1990s. But our play has
too often been predictable and unimaginative, with players
conforming to a pre-agreed game plan rather than weighing
up options for themselves. The players have at times looked
over-coached.

The job of coaching can get harder rather than easier as the
coach gets more established in a job. While almost any team
will respond to a new coach, a change of routine and some
new ideas, it is much more of a challenge to keep players
stimulated once familiarity has set in. This was a problem for
Alan Davies in his last year or so in charge. We had become
so used to him and had gone through so many possible moves
with him that there was a danger we would stop thinking.
Alan recognised this danger and was always careful to drum
into us that 'The moves we have discussed are only options.
I want you to think for yourselves rather than automatically
do what we have discussed.'

There is no doubt Wales has made progress under Graham
Henry. The trouble is that it has been no faster, and in some
cases slower, than other countries. Given our advantages in
resources we should be able to beat Ireland and Scotland
more often than not. That is not happening at the moment,
and recently we have seen Ireland emerging as a team
playing with real confidence, imagination and a belief in what
they are doing. We have now taken two consecutive heavy
beatings by England. While the Cardiff defeat in 2001 reflected some exceptional play by England, who might have

beaten anybody in the world on that form, it is disappointing that the gap seems to be widening rather than closing. At least we seem to be making ground on the French, although that fixture seems to be becoming as odd as the Ireland match, with heavy home defeats alternating with wins in Paris. The 2001 Six Nations game in Paris, after a terrible start, was an occasion when we did play with some freedom and saw players like Rob Howley and Scott Quinnell showing imagination and using their skills to attack the opposition, but that is still too much the exception rather than the rule.

We have often failed to make the best of the talent at our disposal – and I'm not necessarily harking back to players like Leigh Davies here, but regulars like Rob Howley. Like everyone else in Wales I was disappointed and worried by the decline in Rob's play over a couple of years, culminating in him being left out for a time in 2000, and was delighted to see him back to something like his old self in 2001. I think the injury he suffered on the 1997 Lions tour was a more telling blow than most people thought. Serious injuries are often like that. However good you are feeling physically and however keen you are to get back into the game, there is still a mental block which can take a long time to get over. And the longer it takes, the harder it gets.

I thought it was a bad decision to make Rob captain of the side. He was still struggling to get back to his best form after the injury, and what the team needed more than anything else was for him to be able to concentrate on that rather than coping with the extra pressures that go with the captaincy. It gave him added baggage when he did not need it. My choice for the job would have been Scott Gibbs. I know that Scott was not that keen on the job, but he was the best candidate available. As we all know from the 1997 Lions tour, he is a natural leader, and he has since done the job very well for Swansea. Instead, Rob was asked to take it on when he should have been focusing on playing his own game to the best of his ability.

Defences have tightened considerably in the last three or four years. Rob's greatest asset is that he is a terrific runner who can break any defence on his day. But recently openings have been fewer than they were, and we were not making the most of the opportunities that were still there. If you have a scrum with a good right shoulder – and our scrum has been as good as anybody's over the last couple of years – and your back-row forwards stay down, there should be opportunities for a runner as strong as Rob to make breaks. Instead, Wales were looking to the number eight to pick up and pop off a pass, or go by himself, or to Rob to move the ball on to Neil Jenkins. Rob is a strong character and I don't believe he would not get the ball most of the time if he told Scott Quinnell he wanted it. The fact that this strength simply was not used, not just for a single game but over a period of a couple of years, leads me to believe that Rob and Wales were playing to orders, doing what had been decided beforehand rather than using their own initiative and judgement. If so, it was a waste of one of our major assets.

With Rob making fewer breaks, greater focus, and some criticism, has fallen on other aspects of his game such as his passing and kicking. Perhaps they had been neglected a little, because other aspects of his game had been so important to Wales, but I have never seen Rob Howley as a poor passer – quite the opposite. People had talked about Rob's tendency to take steps before passing the ball, but my impression was that that also was not his decision, but something he had been told to do. Henry's idea appeared to be that this would pull defenders in and create space out wide. I have always thought that you would be better off winning and moving the ball quickly to where the space is, so that you get one or two players running at one or two rather than six against six. Whatever the theory was, it did not work for us and we always seemed to be attacking on a narrow front, unable to make much impression. There was little momentum in our game and little variety. The contrast is with Ireland since Peter Stringer and Ronan O'Gara came into the side. They have moved the ball quickly, putting it in front of the men in midfield who were in a position to make breaks.

Having said that Rob was the wrong choice for captain, I thought his removal was handled extremely badly, and it clearly left the man very unhappy. When he was dropped from the team I was staggered that Richard Smith, who had been on the bench since the start of the season, was overlooked in favour of a recall for Rupert Moon. I knew Richard as a young player at Bristol. He is extremely likeable and very talented. There is no doubt that he is an exceptionally good club player who works very hard at his game. I don't know if he would make an international player – there would be some doubts over his consistency – but the only way to find out would be to play him from the start in an international. It was extraordinary that the opportunity was not taken. A replacement, particularly one in a specialist position like scrum-half, must be someone you would be prepared to see on the pitch from the first few minutes of the game if your starter gets injured. Graham Henry had entrusted that role to Richard Smith, so I cannot understand why he was not prepared to start him when he decided to drop Rob. I happened to speak to Richard's father shortly after it happened and he said he was devastated and could not understand why it had been done.

Picking Rupert was a backward step, although I suppose you have to say that he did the job asked for: we won a couple of matches, albeit with some not very pretty rugby. Henry, at the end of the 1999/2000 season, was obviously more concerned with getting a couple of decent results than with our long-term development. Perhaps you cannot blame coaches for doing that when you consider the pressure they are under from the union, the public and the media, but part of the idea behind giving him a five-year contract was surely to free him from that sort of pressure, so that he could think long-term and leave some decent structures behind him. At least in 2001 we saw Gareth Cooper coming onto the bench and making a fine debut against Italy. His try means Gareth is one Wales scrum-half who won't have people criticising his scoring rate – for a while at least.

Graham Henry's handling of Arwel Thomas has also been puzzling, and I believe has undermined Arwel. I do not believe that this has been intentional, but it has had an adverse effect. As we know from some of Arwel's performances for both Swansea and Wales, he can do things and find angles few other players can. At his best he is a danger to any defence in the world. When things go wrong for Arwel, he is told that he needs to go away and work on his defence or do weights to get bigger and stronger. This is missing the point completely. Arwel's problems are to do with confidence. If he is encouraged and his talents are nurtured, he blossoms. But he needs to be on a high, which is hard to maintain across the length of a nine-month season. I sometimes think it would suit Arwel if the season lasted four or five months instead. Arwel takes criticism very much to heart and it undermines him. Not comments by fans or the press, but from people within the game, those whose opinions really matter. Some people might say this indicates that he is not tough enough for top-class rugby. I disagree with that. A good coach needs to be able to deal with people as individuals and to nurture talents as distinctive as Arwel's. To be fair, Arwel has always been in direct competition with Neil Jenkins. They cannot both be at outside-half in the Wales team, but I see no reason why they should not both be incorporated into the squad structure. Leaving Arwel out altogether is a waste of talent we can scarcely afford.

Choosing between the two if they are both at the very peak of their game would be extremely tough, but I would probably have to go for Neil because of the way he strikes fear into opposing teams. You would not call him a rugby genius, but he is an enormously effective player. Before games against Pontypridd and, more recently, Cardiff – it still does not seem natural to see Neil in Cardiff colours – you were always afraid of him because you knew his goalkicking would punish the slightest indiscipline. Neil went through a spectacular patch of scoring in 1999 during the ten-match winning run under Graham Henry which was the basis for his current status as the world record points scorer, but I still do not believe we have used him to the best advantage over the years.

The tendency has been to say to him, 'Neil, you are the greatest kicker in the world. That is what we want you to do for Wales.' But he is also an excellent passer of the ball, and that quality has not been used nearly enough. Given that we have been capable of winning good set-piece ball in recent years, more quick ball should have been going rapidly from Rob Howley to Neil so that he can use his passing skills to put the men outside him into space in the same way that O'Gara launches the Irish centres or Jonny Wilkinson and Mike Catt get England moving. Mark Taylor has one of the best outside breaks in European rugby, but you would hardly know it from our failure to make use of this ability over the last couple of years. Neil has had a terrific career and has done a marvellous job for Wales, but he could have done even more had he been encouraged to use his full range of skills.

Graham Henry evidently has not rated Arwel. One explanation for this looks to be the traditional New Zealand emphasis on size. You can get away with being small at scrum-half there, but they are never too keen on small players in other positions. Shane Williams has also suffered from this philosophy. But not wanting to use Arwel deprived us of potential variety and options during the 1999 World Cup. One test of a coach is how he uses his bench. The match against Australia was one where it was clear Wales were not going to break through, but they had no options on the bench to try to change the pattern. Had Arwel been on the bench he might just have been able to unsettle the Australians. There was no guarantee of this, of course – Australia coped with everything that was thrown at them during the World Cup – but there was absolutely nothing to lose in a match we were clearly losing anyway.

You could look at Arwel's recall for the internationals in the autumn of 2000 two ways. One was that Graham Henry was acknowledging that Arwel had been playing some awesome rugby in the Heineken Cup for Swansea, when he destroyed Wasps and Stade Française, while Neil had not been at his best for Cardiff. The other was that he was bowing to public opinion. Arwel knew he was on trial, that he probably did not have the full confidence of his coach, all of which made it difficult for him to relax into the role.

The way in which Arwel was handled during this period was strange. After playing him against both Samoa and the USA in November 2000 – and he played well twice, Wales winning both games handsomely, although some of Henry's comments about Arwel sounded pretty grudging; he described his play as 'adequate' after one of the matches – it was bizarre then to drop him for the match against South Africa. Arwel should have started against South Africa instead of being demoted to the bench. But then, once Neil had started and was playing extremely well, it was daft to take him off and send Arwel on for the last twenty minutes with the words, 'Go on Arwel, win us the match.' Talk about putting unfair pressure on the man, especially considering that we had fallen behind at the time and the Springboks were starting to look stronger anyway. There are times to use replacements and times to keep players who have started on the pitch. It is a matter of judgement, not pre-arrangement. Graham Henry got it wrong against South Africa and Arwel took most of the blame for the defeat.

I hope that we have not seen the last of Arwel at international level. When the story about Neil's possible retirement broke earlier this year, I was called by a radio station who asked me about the possible candidates for the Welsh number ten shirt. The talk was mostly about Gavin Henson, who had an extraordinary season and has every chance of being a major figure in British rugby over the next decade, but I said that we should not yet write off Arwel. He is still only 26, an age when he should be coming to his peak. There is a huge talent there to be nurtured for the benefit of Wales as well as Swansea, if we care to do it. Toulouse clearly had no doubts about his ability to cope with the demands of the French championship, one of the toughest in the world, when they invited him to sign for them.

There are still two seasons to go until the next World Cup in 2003, and that, rather than now, will be the time to pass a complete judgement on Graham Henry. Any judgement at the moment is an interim one. Over the next two seasons I hope to see players like Gavin Henson, Gareth Cooper, Jamie Robinson and the Neath prop forward Duncan Jones, who impresses me enormously every time I see him play, establishing themselves as international players. Wales should be playing not only with organisation and commitment, but with freedom, skill and imagination.

Graham Henry's job is not only to restore the fortunes of the Welsh team, but to leave us with a structure for success. I am not completely convinced by the large coaching team he is building around him; we seem to be far too prepared to imitate what other countries, in this case England, are doing rather than trying to work out a structure that suits us. Nigel Walker's appointment as development manager should be a good thing, provided he is allowed to do the same sort of job that Alun Davies does with the national elite squad and is not drawn into being yet another backs coach. Given the importance of developing structures, a clear route that can be travelled by the talented young player from school into the senior game and on to the Wales team, it is disappointing that Henry has shown so little active interest in the work of the Dragons Rugby Trust.

I do not believe that he should have been appointed coach of the 2001 British Lions. There are two reasons for this. One is that an appointment to coach the Lions is the pinnacle for a British coach in the same way as playing for them is the ultimate for a player. While you could argue that Welsh rugby was in such disarray at the time of Henry's appointment that we had to have an outsider come in and sort us out, I do not believe you can say the same about British rugby as a whole.

As I said at the discussion session at Paul Arnold's benefit function in the Grand Theatre, ironically enough with

Graham Henry sitting on the same panel, I would have chosen Clive Woodward. I know that this would not have been popular in Wales, but I admire what Clive has achieved with England. He has developed a team playing the sort of rugby we have always admired in Wales, adding imagination and variety to the organisation and forward power England have had for years. He has been prepared to encourage players like Jonny Wilkinson, Mike Catt and Iain Balshaw to use their skills and vision to create space and danger. Catt, in particular, has shown the skills I hope to see in young Welsh players. He can play in a number of positions, has terrific vision and is capable of throwing the long, flat passes in front of a runner that break defences and put the men outside him into space.

It took Woodward a while to get the mix right, but from the start he seemed to me to have the right philosophy. England have had the players for the last ten years but were never prepared to allow them to express themselves. Their national game was all about power; footballing skills came a long way behind. It is typical of Woodward's approach that where previous England coaches were reluctant to play Neil Back because they were afraid that he was too small and lacked the power they wanted, Woodward backed him from the start because his pace and footballing abilities gave England an extra dimension. I played in the same Barbarians side as Back against South Africa in 1994. He was a scrum-half's dream of a back-row forward, always positive and creative and winning a great deal of ball. But it took England another three years and the appointment of Woodward to realise what anyone who had played alongside Back knew years before.

The England back row are a terrific blend. Back might not be that physical, and Richard Hill, a seriously underrated player, might not be the most powerful loose forward in the world, but their skills and those of Lawrence Dallaglio are complementary and go to make up a magnificent combination. On top of that, look at the contribution even a big man like Martin Johnson is making with the ball in his hands. I do not believe England's players are any more naturally talented than our own, but at the moment it is them, not us, playing the sort of rugby we once regarded as our greatest strength.

Clive Woodward's remarkable stewardship of the England side in recent years is not the only reason for thinking that Graham Henry should not have done the Lions job. One of the other possible candidates was Ian McGeechan, who has already been on three Lions tours. Nobody knows more than Ian about the demands such tours make on coaches. He was asked to go again, but he declined, saying he could not afford the time as he had to devote his energies to his job as national coach of Scotland. That should tell us something. The Welsh Rugby Union surely gave a lucrative five-year contract to Graham Henry on the understanding that his sole focus during that time would be the improvement of Welsh rugby, yet they have allowed him to take on something as massively time- and energy-consuming as coaching the Lions. One consequence of this is that he has missed the Wales develop-ment tour to Japan. There was an argument at the time that this entitled the WRU to look at a possible successor to Henry as national coach, but with Lyn Howells, who left the Wales set-up after the tour, in charge even this opportunity was squandered.

Graham Henry should surely have gone to Japan to look at Welsh players of the immediate future, getting to know them better and giving them the benefits of his expertise as a coach through the sort of extended contact that is not normally possible during the regular season. Instead, he chose to go to Australia with the Lions, a tour which inevitably brought back vivid memories from my own playing career.

# **10** The Lions and the Southern Nations

'Everything was done on an informal basis. It was Clive's style as manager. He was incredibly down to earth and disciplined. He did not lay down the law or threaten to throw people off the tour. If there was a problem, he did not pull aside whoever was creating the difficulty and lecture him; instead, he took him to the bar for a quiet chat to sort things out. Any potential difficulties were thus sorted out as soon as they arose, rather than being left to fester. It was an important lesson for any touring team, but not every team I toured with learned it.'

The boys all got together, from all parts of the land,
To set off for Australia, we were a merry band.
We were known as the British Lions, a side of illustrious
    names
Who were going for one reason: to win all of our games.
We arrived one night in Perth, our tour was underway,
And after some light training, our manager had his say.
He stressed that we were Lions and our badge would pull
    us through,
And although we did some giggling, we all knew it was
    true.

I MUST ADMIT that I was no great threat to Dylan Thomas.
But then, from what I've heard of him, he would not have
made much of a scrum-half, although he might have
enjoyed some of the social aspects of a British Lions rugby
tour in the late 1980s. That poem is still among my press
cuttings and souvenirs from the 1989 tour of Australia,
written on the stationery of a succession of hotels we stayed
in during the tour. In the end it grew to fifty verses, telling
the story of our experiences in Australia, all part of the
memories of nine weeks which were among the highlights of
my career.

The letter telling me I had been chosen did not have to
come far to get to Trebanos. It was mailed on 21 March 1989
from Upper Cwmtwrch, just a few miles up the valley, by my
father-in-law Clive Rowlands, who was manager of the tour.

As it happens, I was not at home to receive it. The news of my selection, along with Ieuan, John Devereux, Mike Hall and several other members of the Wales team, reached me, ironically enough, in Australia where we had gone to play in a sevens tournament. We had just beaten England in the Five Nations to see off the threat of our first ever whitewash, for a year at least, and were enjoying the relaxed atmosphere following that reprieve. We were obviously delighted, but one of the things I most remember is how disappointed Phil Davies, a good friend who had had a good year and was a terrific player at his best, was to have missed out.

Clive was right, as he so often is, about the meaning of that badge. To play for the Lions had always been one of my ambitions. It is the next thing you hope for after playing for your country, proving yourself to be one of the best in your position in Britain and Ireland. To be recognised in that way was a wonderful feeling. It made me a member of the best team I ever played in, and led to the single incident which is most remembered from my sixteen and a half years in senior rugby.

Everything felt right from the moment we arrived at our hotel that May, the Oaklands Park at Weybridge in Surrey. I arrived with a few of the Welsh lads, then the Scots, including our captain Finlay Calder, Gavin Hastings and John Jeffrey, turned up. Dean Richards and Mike Teague were among the Englishmen there, and there were three Irishmen: Donal Lenihan, Brendan Mullin and Steve Smith, who was reserve hooker (Paul Dean was injured very early on and had to go home). That sense of four national groups, men who were usually opponents on the field of play, coming together with a single purpose added to the feeling of excitement.

I was rooming with Mike Teague from Gloucester, whom I knew as a tough, highly committed and competitive opponent. I now discovered that he was also one of the world's great snorers, and spent one night in the bathroom in a desperate attempt to get away from the incredible noise and get some sleep. Within a couple of days, though, he felt like a colleague, and so did the rest of the squad. It was fascinating getting to know them all. I already knew Dean Richards was a great number eight with a superb rugby brain; I now found out about the relaxed, laid-back, quietly spoken character who had possibly the worst dress sense in international rugby.

The style of the party was defined from the start. On the first Saturday night we got together for a few drinks. In fact, it was quite a session, with the Four Nations committee picking up the tab. Those few hours brought us together more as a party than a couple of weekends would have done without a session. Finlay set up a series of committees to organise different aspects of the tour. I was one of the senior professionals along with Bob Norster, a small group of the more experienced players, who got together informally to discuss how the tour was going and what we needed to do to improve. Everything was done on an informal basis. It was Clive's style as manager. He was incredibly down to earth and disciplined. He did not lay down the law or threaten to throw people off the tour. If there was a problem, he did not pull aside whoever was creating the difficulty and lecture him; instead, he took him to the bar for a quiet chat to sort things out. Any potential difficulties were thus sorted out as soon as they arose, rather than being left to fester. It was an important lesson for any touring team, but not every team I toured with learned it.

Ian McGeechan was one of the best coaches I have ever played for. He is quietly spoken and has an incredible knowledge and understanding of the game. It certainly helps that he played international rugby and was a Lion himself. You don't have to have been a skilful player to be an effective coach, but it does help. Someone with Ian's experience sees the game differently and more clearly than someone who has none. I don't think it's a fluke that Scotland, with Ian and Jim Telfer as the key influences, have been good at making the most of their resources in recent years, encouraging a player like Gregor Townsend to express his skills in the knowledge that although he will have the occasional bad game, he will win matches you would otherwise lose when he is on form. While Arwel Thomas, who has similar gifts, knows that one bad game will get him slung out of the Wales team, Scotland have persevered with Gregor and been rewarded for that faith. You can argue that Scotland have fewer players and therefore fewer options, but the real difference has been in approach, not resources.

Ian did not dictate to us. Everyone had his say. I had as much input as someone like Bob Norster; Steve Smith, our reserve hooker, had as much to say as I did. Ian wanted everybody to be involved, to be able to work closely together. It worked. At no time on that tour did I feel I was playing away from my strengths or doing things because I had been told to do them. Ian McGeechan and Finlay Calder knew they had the best players in the British Isles in their squad and allowed them to be themselves rather than try to fit them into a preconceived pattern.

I have never felt so relaxed. For nine weeks we were away from the pressures of playing in Wales and from the need to earn a living. We were, in effect, full-time professionals. But it was only for nine weeks, and I knew that it was an exceptional time – at the end of it I had a job and family responsibilities to go back to in Wales. There were distractions, of course. People would ring you at the hotel wanting to know if you were related to them – there are a lot of Joneses around in Australia as well – or if you knew relatives of theirs in Wales. Wherever you go on a Lions tour, you can be sure you will be greeted at the airport by people from the local Welsh society, probably with a choir and one of the older members dressed in Welsh national costume. I was always amazed that people could move thousands of miles, make a new life for themselves in a different country and still feel more Welsh than ever. But I never felt any pressure from this.

I also realised the quality of the players we had in the squad. I remember thinking, 'I can't wait to play with this team. They are going to be so good to play with.' It was always likely that I would be the number one scrum-half. Gary Armstrong is a terrific player, very strong and competitive, but he had only just come into the Scotland team. I also had a sense that Ian particularly wanted some of my strengths in the team.

We started well. Western Australia aren't the strongest state by any means, but we still did well to beat them by a healthy margin. The big games before the first test were against Queensland at Ballymore – where we won, and I was very happy personally with the way I had played – and New South Wales. That match was moved a couple of times because of the weather, and we ended up at the North Sydney Oval, a lovely ground which is also used for cricket. Nick Farr-Jones was playing for them, Phil Kearns was there in one of his first games, and we knew how important it was to beat them – which we did, with a late drop goal by Craig Chalmers.

Having beaten the two states which made up the Australian team, we were confident of winning the first test at the Sydney Football Stadium on 1 July, but we were beaten convincingly, 30–12. I have watched the match on film several times since and they were sharper, quicker in thought and scored some excellent tries. Perhaps we were over-confident. The defeat put us under a lot of pressure. We had believed that we could win the first test, and we still thought we could win the series, but now there was no room for any more slip-ups.

The midweek team, which had become known as Donal's Doughnuts, got us back on track. This was a unique tour in my experience, with no feeling of 'us and them' between the test team and the rest – and I am not just saying that because I was in the test team. There was an extraordinarily strong sense of togetherness and unity in the party. The midweek team developed this very strong and positive identity around Donal Lenihan, who did a very important job for the team as a whole. At the end of the tour he had T-shirts with 'Donal's Doughnuts' printed on them, and I remember Gary Armstrong passing me in the corridor of the hotel and saying, 'You'll never have one of these, Jonesy.' We badly needed them to beat Australian Capital Territory in the match between the first two tests, and they were cheered off by all the test players when they did it.

The second test was back at Ballymore in Brisbane, scene of a few of the highs and lows of my career already: it was where I had scored against England in the World Cup quarter-final in June 1987 and where Wales had taken the first of our trio of beatings by the All Blacks. All through that week before the match, Ian McGeechan was playing mind games with me. He kept on reminding me how important Nick Farr-Jones, their scrum-half and captain, was to them. He was the key influence in their team, the man who called the shots and made things happen. He was also extremely good at influencing referees, chatting to them, saying things like, 'Sir, sir, wasn't he offside?' We had the feeling that if we could knock him off his game, it would knock Australia off as well.

What happened with Nick Farr-Jones in the first few minutes of that second test is something I am still asked about twelve years on.

On the morning of the match, 8 July, I got up, dressed in number ones – the blazer, shirt and tie in which we went to the matches – and watched the first test again on video. I don't think I have ever been so wound up before a match, and that was before Finlay's special line in pre-match oratory which I knew from my experience with Scotland's sevens squad was likely to have you bursting with adrenalin for the first few minutes. I was aching to get to grips physically with Farr-Jones.

An opportunity came at the first scrum. There was nothing premeditated in the sense that I had decided exactly what to do beforehand, but I had gone out with the intention of doing something to unsettle him. It was a spur-of-the-moment decision to stand on his foot at the first scrum and push down. He came back at me, and within seconds there was a pretty lively punch-up going on. Before the match Finlay had emphasised that we were not to take a backward step, that we would tackle hard, put on physical pressure up front, ruck hard and drive the line-out. I knew that if there was any trouble, four men would come instantly to my assistance: Mike Teague, the Gloucester builder, and the three police-men Paul Ackford, Wade Dooley and Dean Richards. And that is exactly what happened.

This punch-up set the tone for the match. Nick was very upset by the incident and kept chatting to the referee. The Australians in general were upset about our physical ap-proach – David Campese is still complaining about it a dozen years later – and it has to be said things got quite brutal at times. Anyone caught on the wrong side of a maul was treated as the All Blacks have been treating opponents for years. There were a few incidents which were rather over the top; at one point David Young stamped on somebody's head, which as anyone who knows Dai will tell you is totally out of character for him. Unfortunately, that is the sort of thing that tends to happen when a team is extremely fired up.

It was not pretty. Today, I would probably have been dismissed and suspended for six to twelve weeks for what I did, but not in 1989. I can't say that I regret it, though. It probably was the turning point of the match and the series. Nick Farr-Jones was distracted from his normal game and was not nearly as effective as he had been the week before. Dealing with a player who tries to take you on physically may not be one of the most attractive aspects of rugby, but it is part of the game and you have to be able to do it. I'd had a couple of rough games against Richard Hill when he was playing for England. From Jerry Guscott's account it sounds as though all Richard wanted to do before the games was kill me, but then that was his style. The important thing is not to allow yourself to be distracted and dragged away from playing your natural game, which is what happened to Farr-Jones.

We won that game 19–12 and established something of a physical and psychological edge over the Aussies. It was one of those occasions – there were rather too few of them in my career for my liking – when the pack gave me an 'armchair ride', which is much more comfortable than the ride I was becoming used to playing for Wales.

We were fired up for the third test as well. In the first few minutes we were awarded a scrum and Farr-Jones refused to let me have the ball. I tried to butt him – something else which would get me six to twelve weeks nowadays – but only managed to split my own eye open. Perhaps I was not that well suited to this style of rugby after all! The game is remembered for the late try Ieuan scored to win the match by one point, and the series. We knew that while David Campese was a great winger who loved having the ball in front of him, he was vulnerable and liable to make a mistake if you put the ball behind him. That is what happened: he got himself in a bit of a tangle with Greg Martin and Ieuan scored the try. It was also a great example of Ieuan's strength and confidence, though. He put the pressure on Campo and was good enough to take advantage when that pressure paid off.

I had an extremely scary moment right at the end of the match. We knew we were in injury time when we were awarded a scrum in their 25. This left me with a decision to make: kick to touch and risk their winning the ball from the line-out, or try a box-kick into the in-goal area and hope it ran dead? I went for the box-kick, but their winger Ian Williams, who was extremely fast, caught it cleanly and set off on a counter-attack. For a moment he had space out wide, we were struggling to get defenders across and I was thinking I'd kicked the series away in the last seconds. To my intense relief Scott Hastings then got across and put in a tackle, and soon afterwards the referee blew the whistle. But for a moment we all had visions of them scoring a hundred-yard try and snatching away the series win we had worked so hard for.

My second confrontation with Nick Farr-Jones had an odd sequel later that night. After the dinner, Farr-Jones's wife, who was pretty upset about what I had done to her husband, was complaining about the way we had played and saying what a thug I was (I suppose Meg would have said much the same about anyone who had done the same to me). Gary Armstrong, who had had a few drinks by then, got involved in the discussion with her and they ended up having quite a row. Gary, who had become a good friend of mine, got very upset about it and was close to tears.

My second Lions tour, to New Zealand in 1993, was a much less happy and rather frustrating experience. To start with I only made the party when Gary Armstrong got injured. I was out of the Wales team at the time, but all the talk had been that Gary and I would be the scrum-halves and I had mistakenly half-assumed it was a formality. On the day when the letters should have arrived there was no news, so I rang Dai Richards, who was one of the selectors. He told me that Dewi Morris had been selected along with Gary, and that I was on stand-by. I asked Dai why I had been left out. He said Dewi had been playing well for England – which he certainly had – and that they had timed his pass against mine and found he was as quick, which I must admit came as a surprise to me. I was too devastated to ask much more. It was one of the greatest disappointments of my career, one of the times when I did a lot of talking with Geoff, who knew to expect a call when something like this happened, or would make the call first himself.

But Gary's misfortune – he had a serious groin injury and was advised that he must have an operation which meant missing the tour – was my good luck. I was called up, and on arrival in New Zealand I heard a radio interview with John Hart in which he said he thought I was one of the players likely to have a big influence on the series. I played in the first match against North Auckland, which went reasonably well personally but was not a great team performance. Dewi played in the next match. He played well, and it was a better all-round team effort. He was also the original selection for the tour, so he had an advantage and it was clear I was going to have to play very well to get into the test team.

I could not have played in the first test in Christchurch on 12 June anyway. I was ill and, for once, sitting on that bench, I was hoping I would not have to go on. There was no way I was fit to play; had I had to go on early, it would have been disastrous. The Lions lost narrowly, 20–18, and after that I had one chance to play myself into the test team: the midweek game against Southland. It did not go that well, and Dewi then had an excellent game in Wellington where we won the second test 20–7, so he was always going to play in the third at Eden Park.

Playing for the midweek side was not a pleasant experience. There was nothing like the Donal's Doughnuts phenomenon this time round. The team had no real identity and it effectively fell apart as the tour went on. The tour management has to take a lot of the blame for this. There was a very clear 'us and them' feeling in the party from early on. In 1989 the management would have done something about this; in 1993 it was allowed to fester. Gavin Hastings, who was captain, was completely focused on the test matches and Geech, who was coach again, had handed the midweek team over to Dick Best. Geoff Cooke, who was the manager, was very little help. It even reached the point where the test and midweek teams were segregated, staying in different wings of the same hotel.

Before our match against Waikato, Geoff read out the names of those in the team, then said to the test team regulars, 'Look, I know you don't want to have to sit on the bench, but somebody has to.' As he read out the names of those detailed to sit on the bench, the other test players laughed at their colleagues' fate. Richard Webster, who always says what he thinks, stood up and told them he thought their attitude was disgraceful.

There was animosity between the two squads from quite early on, and again the management did little or nothing to address the problem. After one training session we were kept waiting on the coach for half an hour while the test team finished. We were all pretty fed up about this. Mike Teague and Webby were sitting at the back with a bag full of lemons and oranges and when the test team got on they were barraged with the fruit. On another occasion Webby said to Nick Popplewell that it was 'nice to see him getting a game as a guest with Geoff Cooke's England team'.

The midweek team simply fell apart through disillusionment. It threw the towel in. There was a lot of talk about the Scottish front five not being up to it, which was unfair to Kenny Milne, whom I always rated as a good hooker, and Paul Burnell, who also kept on battling. And early in the tour I had been very impressed by Damian Cronin. Looking at him in training I thought he was a forward who had everything and would certainly challenge for the test team. But one of the dangers of tours is the amount of food you have available day and night. Damian, who was big anyway, lost his self-discipline when he was disappointed and ate enormous amounts. He must have gained about two stone by the end of the tour.

In that match at Waikato, we took a real beating. Our scrum was going backwards at an incredible rate and the next thing I knew Peter Wright, the prop on my side and roughly parallel with me, had popped his head out and was trying to guard the blindside as the scrum rocketed backwards. He simply could not handle the pressure. I was put in mind of the time Peter Francis of Maesteg, an excellent club prop, played against Scotland at Murrayfield. He could not cope then and our scrum was a terrible mess, so much so that the referee had said to Bob Norster, 'I'm not very happy with your tighthead.' All Bob could say was, 'You're unhappy, ref? How do you think I feel about it?'

Still, there were those who tried their best to the end. Will Carling, with whom I always got on – he got on with most of the Welsh lads in spite of the image he had with people who did not know him – kept on battling. Stuart Barnes was unlucky. He might have played in the test matches, but I trod on his head in the match against Southland and split it open. We had been practising rucking all week, and Stuart said afterwards that it was just his luck that while our pack did not know how to ruck, I did! Stuart was a hugely gifted natural player who lived life to the full on and off the field. Rugby was important to him, but it was not the be all and end all. Not many people know more about New Zealand red wine than he did by the end of that tour. Mike Teague and Webby never gave up either, and we at least got some entertainment from the relationship between Webby and Dick Best, a real love-hate relationship which concealed a fair bit of mutual respect.

Webby is loud, boisterous, a real character, while Dick is laid-back and has a lovely dry sense of humour. On one occasion Webby asked if he was going for a drink that evening and Dick said, 'Richard, I would rather stick pins in my eyes.' Webby was always saying that Dick would have to come for a drink next time he was in Swansea, and Dick said, 'I would love to come and meet your father. I would love to meet the man who produced you.' Webby played well on tour – he was unlucky that he had to compete with Peter Winterbottom for a test place – but he was another who couldn't resist the food. By the end of the tour, he was borrowing Damian Cronin's clothing. Dick didn't miss this, and quipped on one occasion, 'Richard, when you get back to Swansea, they'll paint you white, put wheels on you and use you as a sightscreen.' Dick gave us another humorous moment before the second test, when we discovered that he had backed the All Blacks in a sweep held by some of the hotel staff, the press and the management. He was hauled up in front of the tour court for betting against his own team and had to come and defend himself.

But overall it was a frustrating experience, completely different to 1989, and not just because I wasn't in the test team this time round. I have little doubt the 1989 management would have sorted out the problems their 1993 counterparts simply dismissed. For all that, though, I would not have missed the experience.

And I am keen that other players, from Wales and the other home nations, continue to have that experience. To lose the

Lions as an experience, as the highest aspiration for British and Irish rugby players, would be a disaster. I am delighted that they have survived into the professional era when many critics were predicting their demise. They thought the Lions were a thing of the past, but they couldn't have been more wrong. The southern unions may occasionally question the value of some international matches, but you will never hear them decry matches involving the Lions. They and their fans regard a visit by the Lions as an attraction second to none in the game, as special occasions to be cherished – as do Welsh fans, who travel in support of the tour in huge numbers. To me, the Lions will always be about the future, the biggest thing in our game and the ultimate target for our best young players. The current four-year cycle, meaning that the Lions visit each of the three great southern-hemisphere rugby nations once every twelve years, works well. You would not want it to be any more frequent than that, now that the four-year World Cup cycle, with which it alternates, is established in its own right. It means that every other year British and Irish players have something to aim for beyond a Six Nations programme.

There is a magic about the Lions that nothing else quite matches. For the individual, a Lions tour offers one of the greatest prizes in the game: the chance to step up from being the best in your country to being the best in Britain and Ireland, and to play with others who are judged to be in the same category in their positions. It is a real experience to be surrounded by players who by definition are of higher quality than the average international player. It cannot fail to make you a better player. But although this challenge of proving yourself the best in your position makes the Lions an attraction in itself, there is of course more to it than that. A great deal of the appeal comes from the teams you are playing against – the three great powers from the southern hemisphere: New Zealand, South Africa and Australia.

If, like me, you come from a rugby community in Wales, then you grew up on the stories and legends of the past – of great Welsh teams and players, and of the teams they played against. You heard all about the great southern-hemisphere teams from earlier ages, in particular about the All Blacks. When I was a youngster, Australia were not as strong as the All Blacks and Wales normally expected to beat them. They did not host Lions tours until 1989. It was not until their great schoolboy team of the late 1970s developed into their senior Grand Slam touring team of 1984 that Australia were taken as seriously as New Zealand. We also saw and heard less of South Africa, which was isolated due to apartheid. Wales did not play the Springboks between 1970, when Gareth Edwards scored an equalising try in a mudbath at the Arms Park, and 1994.

So the All Blacks were the most important part of our world-view of rugby. As a youngster I always had a Wales shirt, but I also owned an All Black shirt (no, not Neath!). I learned about a rivalry between two countries which were at opposite ends of the world but which had roughly the same population, similarities in lifestyle and above all a shared passion for rugby. I heard about the great games played when the All Blacks visited Wales, not least among them Llanelli's stunning victory in 1972. One of the great thrills of my life to that point was going to Stradey to see Llanelli play the All Blacks, my brother Anthony sitting on the bench for the Scarlets. Then, of course, came my admiration for Dave Loveridge. I could admire Gareth Edwards and Terry Holmes, but never hope to play like them. Loveridge, however, was the perfect model: not very big, but still a great scrum-half whose most important skill was the ability to make space for other people to play in. Exactly the kind of player I wanted to be.

Despite not getting to see the Springboks play during this period, or perhaps because of that, there was a mystique about this country whose rugby was so strong that Wales had never beaten them. South Africa was always in the news for political reasons, which in some ways made it even more fascinating. There was an element of the unknown about it.

I never did get to play for Wales against the Spring-boks, although I helped the French Barbarians beat them in 1992 and captained the Barbarians team which beat them in Dublin in 1994. I was also on the receiving end when they ran riot against Swansea earlier on the same tour. By contrast, I played four times for Wales against the All Blacks and three times against the Wallabies. But it was South Africa that was to have the greatest impact on me, with which country I developed the closest connection.

One of the most controversial events of my career was the tour to South Africa by a World XV in 1989 to celebrate the centenary of the South African Rugby Union, shortly after the Lions tour to Australia had finished. I heard about it initially from Paul Thorburn who said he had been asked to sound out Welsh players who might be interested in going. I told him that I was interested. Having heard so much about South African rugby, I was very keen to play against the Springboks to find out how good they really were. I have never been a particularly political animal myself. I was aware that people I respected, like Clem Thomas and John Taylor, were opposed to contact with South Africa, but I also took the view that they had formed those opinions on the basis of going to South Africa and making their own minds up, and I wanted to have the chance to do that myself. There was also the issue of the money being offered. It was not a massive amount by the standards of modern professional players' salaries, but by the standards of the amateur game – or my own salary at the time – it was a colossal amount, more than two years' pay. An amount like that, I knew, would make a huge difference to my family's life.

It was an officially sanctioned tour. In any case, I did not have to go far to find out the Welsh Rugby Union's position on the tour as this was the year when my father-in-law, Clive Rowlands, was president of the WRU. Clive had declined his invitation to go to South Africa, although most of the committee went, but he told me that the decision as to whether or not I went was entirely up to me. After a meeting with a man named Kobus Coetzee, who came over to talk to the players who had been invited, I agreed to go.

Then the news of the tour hit the press and all hell broke loose. There was talk of protests, of players possibly being banned from St Helen's (which was council-owned), of sanctions against those who went. I went away for the weekend to Bath with Meg and thought about whether I should go or not. I was actually sitting in the bath in our hotel room when I finally made the decision, calling out, 'Meg, I've decided. I'm not going.' I rang Clive and told him what I had decided. He said, 'I'm delighted. I didn't want to press you but I think you have made the right decision.' Tony Clement had been waiting on my decision before he chose whether to go or not. Once I told Clem, we both decided to go and see David East, the secretary of the WRU at the time, and tell him we were not going. He issued a statement to the press about us.

That would probably have been the end of the story had there not been a Welsh squad session the following week in Aberystwyth. When we met up on a Friday all the talk was about who was going, who was not and the amounts of money being offered. A lot of people – Thorby, Mike Hall, Bob Norster and several others – had signed up to go. Those who hadn't been invited had obviously not been told exactly how much was on offer, and when they found out they started asking how on earth I could turn down that sort of money. We all went out for a drink, and as we talked together I started to think again. If there were seven or eight Welsh players going anyway, why shouldn't I go with them? I rang Kobus Coetzee from Aberystwyth and told him that I had changed my mind and was coming after all.

I had spoken to John Ryan and John Dawes before the phone call and they had said, 'It's up to you, your decision entirely. Whatever you do, it won't affect our attitude towards you.' And before going to Aberystwyth I had sounded out Mike James at Swansea Rugby Club, concerned about the possible implications in terms of my relationship with the club – a factor in my original decision to turn the tour down.

Mike had said they would support my right to make a personal decision. David Richards, my boss at work, also told me there was no problem with taking time off to go.

It was a strange day. There were anti-apartheid demonstrators waiting for us at the training facility. They were booing the players who were going and coming over to congratulate me and Clem for refusing. I hadn't the nerve to tell them I had changed my mind and was going after all. I had to tell certain other people, though. Meg was very upset when I rang her – she was in tears on the phone – and I spent a long time trying to contact Clive, who was somewhere in Aberaeron. This was before the days of mobile phones and I tried several times without success. I was not looking forward to telling him, and I must admit that I felt relieved each time I could not get through to him.

On the Sunday there were journalists and television cameras outside the house. Tony Clement, who had also agreed to go after all, and I left early to avoid them and drove to Cardiff airport where a private room had been booked. From there, a helicopter took us to Heathrow. I did not get through to Clive until we were at Heathrow and about to get on to the plane to South Africa. He was understandably upset when I told him the news. He didn't object to my going, but he was upset at the way things had happened. It was extremely embarrassing for him as president of the Welsh Rugby Union. He had been telling everyone that Tony and I were not going, and the union had of course already put out a statement on our behalf. Now we were going after all. He offered to stand down as president of the union as a result of this; thankfully, the WRU made one of its wiser decisions and refused to accept his resignation. I very much regret the embarrassment my actions caused Clive and David East; fortunately, our relationship was not affected.

I can understand why people were angry with us and thought we should not be going, but I do not regret it. Nevertheless, it was a hard decision to make. I wanted to go to South Africa, to see the country for myself and play rugby against the Springboks, and it certainly made a big difference to me financially. The rugby was very enjoyable. Pierre Berbizier played at scrum-half in the first match and I played the second in Pretoria. We were wonderfully looked after the whole time we were there. I had actually expected the segregation to be worse and more complete than it turned out to be, but there were still reminders that we were not in a normal country. In Port Elizabeth there were armed guards in our hotel, and we were not allowed to go anywhere in South Africa without guards. They would come out with us and check the minibus for explosives. In Cape Town one day, we were on our way to one of the townships for a coaching session when we came across a van turned over in the road and several more which had been set alight. The guards said it was too dangerous to go any further, so the minibus turned round and we returned to our hotel.

The 1989 trip was a fairly short one. A longer, more important exposure to South Africa came in 1994, by which time there had been a great deal of political change and the country had been accepted back into international rugby. It all started when I went to Pretoria to play for a World XV captained by Gavin Hastings in a benefit match for Naas Botha. Morne du Plessis had rung me before I went over to say he wanted to meet to talk about me going to play in South Africa. He explained that the Western Province state team had a problem at scrum-half, and they also wanted international players to come in and help in their development work with the non-white population. Morne is a marvellous man and was a great player, so an offer from him was very flattering.

When I went back to Swansea I spoke to my boss at the Swansea Building Society, 'Spider' Davies, who had been the first-choice scrum-half when I started with the All Whites. He said, 'You have to do this. It is an opportunity you can't turn down. You and your family will look back on the experience for ever.' I had to leave my job at the building society – it is a small company and could not afford to have an employee away for several months – but this was not the problem it might have been for me as I was so well looked after by Western Province. They gave me a job as a development officer working with schools and in their community development programme. My travel and living costs were subsidised and Meg, who came out a couple of weeks after I did along with Emily, had an allowance. We had never before been so well off.

Morne and F.C. Smit, a second-row forward who is a bit of a legend in Western Province, picked me up at the airport – literally. I still have the pictures showing me suspended between these two extremely large men. F.C. took me out for the day, showing me all the sights – and there are plenty of them – in and around Cape Town. But if it was an important day for me, it was an even more important one for South Africa. It was late April, and the first fully democratic elections were taking place, as a result of which Nelson Mandela would be elected president. They had been expecting some unrest, but we saw none during our journey around Cape Town and places like Stellenbosch, just the incredible sight of hundreds of people waiting patiently, for the first time in their lives, for their turn to vote.

Provincial rugby in South Africa was certainly a step up, but not the huge one you might expect. It was a little quicker and more physical than I was used to, but there was little or no difference in ability and I quickly felt quite comfortable. I was surprised when South Africa won the World Cup in 1995. I didn't think they quite had the ability to beat Australia and New Zealand, but they did – largely through sheer passion and commitment.

Alongside the rugby, there was of course my work as a development officer for the Western Province Rugby Union, promoting the game in schools. This was not done exclusively in the townships, but that was where the main concentration was. I worked with Geoff Crowster and Norman Mbiko, two of the other development officers. We got an incredibly warm welcome wherever we went; when we arrived at a school all the children and the teachers would be out waiting for us. On the way into the townships I would look at the huts and shacks and wonder how anybody could manage to live in them. Then you'd see the children who came from those shacks, dressed in their spotless clothes, and think of the effort that must have taken in those conditions.

Western Province has a stronger tradition of black and coloured rugby than some other parts of South Africa, so it has a bit of a head start over the other provinces. We had two or three coloured players in the provincial squad. While I was there I was also attached to the University of the Western Cape club, which mainly comprised coloured players. I was only able to play for them once, against Stellenbosch University seconds at Newlands. Stellenbosch seconds were pretty much as good as their firsts, who are always very strong, and they beat us by about seventy points, but it was the first time UWC had played at Newlands. In spite of the result, my team-mates were hugely excited that day, drinking and singing after the game.

I enjoyed my time in Cape Town very much, although both my years there were affected by injury – which is ironic when you consider that I was fortunate with injuries for most of my career. In the first year things went well until I was hurt during a Lion Cup quarter-final against Natal, a very strong side with hugely influential players like Gary Teichmann and Kevin Putt. I tried to come back too soon from my injury and ended up needing a small cartilage operation, which effectively ended my season there. Still, I must have made a good impression because I was asked if I would consider staying in South Africa and qualifying to play for them. Perhaps they felt they were a little short of scrum-halves; Joost van der Westhuizen had only just broken into the Springboks side and there was not a great deal of cover for him. It was a very flattering offer, particularly as I could not get into the Wales side at the time, but I was never going to accept it. I could not play for any country other than Wales. It would feel completely wrong. And much as I liked Cape Town, I did not want to leave Trebanos.

I have very fond memories of South Africa, and our son Tiaan owes his name to our stay there. He is not, however, specifically named after Tiaan Strauss, although he is a good friend; Meg and I simply liked the name. Tiaan was one of a number of players who impressed me enormously with his dedication to the game. While Joel Stransky was, like me, a development officer employed by the Western Province Rugby Union who could devote his whole working life to rugby and rugby-related activities, other players still had jobs. Tiaan was a solicitor, Keith Andrews was an accountant, F.C. Smit was a director of a security company, our big prop Tommie Laubscher was a farmer and Garry Pagel, a prop who has since played for Northampton, managed a garage. Their employers were all flexible about their commitments – one difference between South Africa and Britain is the distances you have to travel to games – but they still had to do their jobs properly and fit rugby around them. Garry, for instance, was often in the gym at five in the morning before starting work at seven. Then at five or six in the afternoon he'd be back in the gym for another session.

One of the things that most impressed me about South African players was their desire to be the best and their willingness to do whatever it took to achieve that. There was a burning desire to play for the Springboks. I think we in Wales can learn from that attitude. We have a tendency to accept second best too readily, to be content to play social rugby rather than stretch ourselves to be the best players we possibly can be. As with New Zealanders, there is an ambition about South African players that drives them to fulfil their potential. We need more of that ambition in Wales.

We can learn from Australia as well. Australia has far fewer professional players than we have – payment for playing does not extend very far beyond the three Super 12 squads – and they play fewer games than we do. From this rather limited base of players, they have won the World Cup twice – and unlike New Zealand and South Africa they have done so without being host nation. One element in this is obviously the attitude and competitiveness of Australian sports people. They over-achieve in almost any sport you can mention, so we should not be too surprised that they are successful at rugby union as well. But I also think the way they play their rugby is important.

That style goes back to the incredible Schools team of the 1970s, the one with the Ella brothers, Andy Slack and a few other people who went on to become world-class senior players. I saw them play Wales Schools because a Trebanos boy, Phil Hamer, had been chosen. They were simply awesome. They were so much in control and in charge, their handling was superb and their back play was far more fluent and dynamic than any Schools team I had ever seen. That approach was carried forward into the senior team, and although every member of that team is now long retired, the style was passed down to the outstanding Australian teams who have succeeded them.

They were one of the first teams to use the inside-centre to complement the outside-half as a decision-maker and game-breaker. This gave them a wider range of attacking options and the opposition a great deal more to worry about, and also took a great deal of pressure off the outside-half. He was still expected to be a creator, but not the only one. It worked superbly in 1984 when they had Mark Ella, who was at his peak, at outside-half and Michael Lynagh, who had only just got into the team, at inside-centre.

Australian back divisions nearly always have several potential game-breakers, all footballers who are capable of playing in more than one position. Stephen Larkham has played at full-back and outside-half, Joe Roff is almost as good in midfield as he is on the wing, Brian Smith played both half-back positions and Matt Burke has switched successfully between wing and full-back. They can make the switch because they have the all-round football skills to change position confidently. Australia cherishes and encourages those skills and the players who have them.

We can and should learn from the example of the southern-hemisphere nations; when they have been so much better than us over the last decade, it would be daft not to try to do so. But we also need to exercise some judgement. The only thing as bad as pretending we have nothing to learn would be to slavishly copy everything they do, assuming that the way they do things is automatically better. There is always a temptation simply to copy whoever is strongest at a particular time, but what happens when somebody else becomes stronger? Do you then change everything again and try to copy the new champions?

It is not so long since the All Blacks were being touted as the example for everyone to follow. That looks a little less convincing now, after New Zealand failed to get a single team into the Super 12 semi-finals in 2001. It will take more than a single bad year to convince me, or anyone else, that New Zealand rugby is about to go into terminal decline, but it has still been interesting to see them asking questions about the way things are done, and experts there suggesting that the system which was supposed to be the model for us all might not be so perfect after all. John Graham, who was Graham Henry's great mentor as a schoolteacher, has argued that New Zealand should withdraw from the Super 12 competition. This suggests that the people in Wales who resisted creating artificial regional teams or amalgamating clubs for European competition – both ideas inspired by the Super 12 – had considerably more of a point than they have been credited with.

It does not necessarily mean that New Zealand is getting anything particularly wrong, either. But it is worth reminding ourselves that neither they, South Africa or Australia necessarily have all the answers, that we should not automatically assume a southern-hemisphere accent equals superior rugby wisdom. It is a matter, as always, of exercising our own judgement. We must always be open to new ideas, ready to question and improve what we are doing. If something or someone from outside can help us, we should not be too proud to look for or accept that help. Australia was not too proud to ask Ray Williams for help when it was in trouble in the 1970s, and when he agreed they listened to him and adapted his ideas to Australian circumstances. That must be our approach. We must always be on the look-out for the best ideas, but be mindful of the fact that they will only be useful if they can be made to work in a Welsh context. Attempts to turn us into an imitation All Blacks simply will not work.

# **11** Allied Trades

'It is important to get ex-players involved in coaching. Being a good player is not an absolute requirement for being a good coach, but it certainly helps. It gives you a feel for the game and an understanding of how it works that is very difficult for a non-player to pick up. It allows you to look at a move on a blackboard, for instance, and say, "It looks as though it should work, but we know from matchday experience that it won't. It should create space in a particular area of the pitch, but unfortunately it never does."'

O NE OF THE MOST FREQUENT sayings about rugby is that it is a players' game – or at least that it should be. They have the central role to which everything else in the game is geared. When we talk about making Welsh rugby great again, we are talking about our players. But, of course, players are not the only people involved in the game, and others have vital roles to play in raising our standards.

Most of those roles are ones to which a player can aspire after he has finished playing. Involvement in the game can last a long time, in some cases a lifetime, after you dump your kitbag in the cupboard under the stairs for the last time. And it can take in a whole range of activities. Take, for example, my father-in-law, Clive Rowlands. He gave up playing more than thirty years ago after captaining Wales in all fourteen internationals he played in. Since then he has been national coach, manager of both Wales and the Lions and president of the Welsh Rugby Union, and he is still working regularly as a broadcaster. Clive Norling was one of the world's top referees, was involved in the management at Bridgend and is now an administrator as the WRU's director of referees. The people in these other roles – coaches, administrators, referees and journalists – have an important influence on the game, for better or worse. What they say and do can affect the game as a whole and individual players.

The influence of, and importance attached to, coaches has grown throughout my time in rugby. The game has changed enormously over the last twenty to thirty years, and the rise of coaches and coaching has been perhaps the greatest change. Wales did not even have a national coach until the mid-1960s – although we were still ahead of the rest of Britain – and Clive was one of the first. That a coach can now be paid £250,000 a year and become a greater national hero than any of his players reflects the scale of the change. Much of this book has concerned itself with different coaches and their individual styles, and with my concerns about the way players – particularly those in the formative years from 16 to 21 – are being coached nowadays.

In those early days, Welsh coaches were regarded as being among the best in the world. The Australians seized on Ray Williams' advice, Clive was a central figure in the successes of the 1970s, Carwyn James became legendary for his work with the 1971 British Lions and Llanelli, and for his remarkable ability to analyse the game. We are still not short of talent. Lyn Jones has done a wonderful job at Neath, Gareth Jenkins' record at Llanelli speaks for itself – and made him a credible candidate to coach the Lions – and I don't need to say anything more about Mike Ruddock's qualities. We need to continue to produce people of this quality, and not just at senior level. The quality of coaches in the schools and club youth sections who play a vital, formative role in the development of young players is equally important. Bad coaching can destroy talent before it gets a chance to blossom.

This is one area where I do believe the Welsh game is in good hands, with the appointment of Mostyn Richards as the WRU's director of development. I have had a great deal to do with Mostyn since his appointment last year, and I have no doubt that he is on the right track. One of the changes since he came in has been the creation of a special Level 4 coaching award, the highest level awarded anywhere in the world. One of the distinctive things about it is that you have to be invited to do it. It is not simply a matter, as with the progression from Levels 1 through to 3, of passing the exams and automatically becoming eligible to take the higher level.

One of the worries about coaching is the extent to which coaches rely on their training, going entirely by the book and expecting to dictate to players everything they should do. I have been at meetings where this point has been raised with Mostyn, and been reassured by his response: he points out that this is bad coaching, that coaches must always allow players to express themselves and take their own decisions on the field. That is the philosophy we need our coaches to follow.

It is important to get ex-players involved in coaching. Being a good player is not an absolute requirement for being a good coach, but it certainly helps. It gives you a feel for the game and an understanding of how it works that is very difficult for a non-player to pick up. It allows you to look at a move on a blackboard, for instance, and say, 'It looks as though it should work, but we know from matchday experience that it won't. It should create space in a particular area of the pitch, but unfortunately it never does.' We also need players from all positions to get involved. There is a limit to what a lock forward can tell you about playing at full-back, or a scrum-half about the front row. This is one reason why we are seeing more specialist-position coaches in the game, and that trend is likely to continue.

Terry Cobner has said to me on several occasions that he would like me to take the different coaching badges. So far it has not been possible – there have been other priorities in my life – but I would not rule out doing it at some time in the future. Some of my colleagues have moved into coaching. Paul Moriarty is still playing at Swansea, but he is also now an assistant coach and the club clearly sees him as one of its coaches of the future. Tony Clement did very well in 2000/01 at Dunvant and certainly has the intelligence and analytical ability to make an excellent coach. Phil Davies, a colleague both for Wales and for a time at work, has done a magnificent job taking Leeds into the English Premiership.

We have an equally strong tradition in refereeing. During my time as a player Clive Norling and Derek Bevan, in their different styles, were regarded as two of the best in the world. Derek is a Vardre boy whose career as a referee is the classic poacher-turned-gamekeeper story. By all accounts he was a pretty physical player who got into a fair amount of trouble with referees, but he took the job up to stay involved in the game after an injury stopped him playing. Derek is perhaps the most consistent of all top referees. He knows the game and the people involved in it and has an excellent eye for the sort of things players try to get away with, perhaps because he remembers trying to get away with them himself. He is not universally loved – he has never been Cardiff's favourite referee, for instance – but you know that when Derek is in charge there is a good chance of a game both the players and spectators will enjoy. He always comes down hard on foul play, but his main aim is to ensure that the game flows. Some of the most enjoyable and exciting games I ever played in were refereed by Derek. He also has an excellent empathy with players. If he makes a decision you do not like or understand you can ask him to explain it without running the risk that he will hold it against you for the rest of the game.

Clive was different in style. You never ever questioned Clive in that way – not if you had any sense, anyway. He dominated games with his personality. You were never in any doubt as to who was in charge. Players were almost afraid of him. Clive could do things other referees would never try, and get away with them because he had such presence and credibility. He once sent off Ian Eidman of Cardiff and Ikey Stephens of Bridgend for persistently collapsing the scrum only a few minutes into a match. I don't believe any other referee would have got away with it, but players accepted it from Clive. He also refereed another match without giving a single penalty, and this was one of his great virtues: he wanted the game played in an open fashion with players allowed to display their attacking skills.

Of course, Clive is now in charge of all referees and refereeing in Wales. It is not a job I envy. He has to set guidelines which suit both the international panel members and also the young referee just starting out who is overseeing Trebanos seconds against Cwmtwrch seconds. Among the current crop, Clive appears to be particularly enthusiastic about Nigel Whitehouse, perhaps because Nigel has first-class playing experience himself as a scrum-half for South Wales Police. Clayton Thomas also played to a decent standard at outside-half. The other panel member is Rob Davies, whose great asset is a bubbly personality and a huge enthusiasm for the game. Rob has an identical twin brother who lives in Swansea. I'm forever bumping into him, saying 'Hello, Rob' and being told 'I'm not Rob.'

While knowledge of the laws is the most basic requirement for a referee, the right personality is just as important. It helps enormously if you are a bit of a character who can get on with players, while staying in control and being wise to the tricks they will try to pull. Good referees have to be able to perform a balancing act between enforcing the rules and keeping the game flowing. If you pull up every possible infringement the game becomes almost unplayable; if you go too far the other way it is just as bad.

Much the same applies to training and assessing referees. Of course we want referees to be consistent, for there to be some basic uniformity in interpretation. But referees have to be able to make their own judgements and develop their own style of refereeing. Clive and Derek were both superb, but in very different ways. If assessors and the people who made appointments had attempted to impose complete uniformity, one or possibly both of them might have been lost to the game – at the top level, at least. Given that Clive was such an individualist himself, you would hope that he would allow other referees to develop their own way of doing things. I am not sure, however, that this is the case.

There seems to me to be too great an emphasis on strict application of the laws, with assessors marking referees harder on this than on whether they develop the sort of empathy with players which keeps games flowing and good-tempered. A lot, of course, depends on the attitude of the players. If they are determined to slow the game down or provoke their opponents into a physical confrontation, the referee has to act firmly to stop them. It will not always work. But a referee who has a feel for the game and a good relationship with players is a vital element in games which allow players to achieve what they are on the field to achieve. Getting that balance right, with referees who know the game and its players as well as they know the rules, is better for players, for spectators and ultimately for the Welsh game as a whole.

Referees, like players, also have to develop the ability to cope with criticism. Coping with the opposing crowd, who will do their level best to put you off, is part of the game. So is coping with the press, which can be much harder to deal with. One of the things I tell the national elite squad players I work with is that it is something they will have to learn to live with, and it is perhaps the toughest part of being a top player. It is never pleasant to be told that you have not played well, particularly if you feel it is not true, and something which is in print for you, your friends, your family and team-mates to see and read is tougher to take than something shouted from the terraces by someone you know is just trying to distract you anyway.

You also learn rapidly who is and is not to be taken seriously. There are some former players who get a call whenever a paper wants to stir up a story, the journalists knowing that they are always prepared to be critical just for the sake of it. You learn after a while to ignore them. There are others who are always worth listening to. From the start of my career I always knew that anything Clem Thomas or Gerald Davies wrote was worth taking seriously. They had both been great players; Gerald was my first hero. It is not absolutely necessary to have played well to be a good journalist – there are people who have learned about the game and brought other abilities to the job – but it does help both in terms of credibility and an instinctive feel for what is happening on the pitch. Gerald and Clem share a deep understanding of the game with first-hand knowledge of what it is like to be a player at club and international level. They know that playing top-class rugby is always tough, and neither has ever been adversely critical just for the sake of it. If they said you had not played well, they always looked for an explanation. They were constructive in their criticism, and it was always worth taking notice of them.

I have very few complaints about the way I was treated by journalists during my career. At the beginning, people like Gerald, Clem, John Billot of the *Western Mail* and Ron Griffiths of the *Evening Post* talked about me as a likely Wales player. Obviously there were times when I was less happy about what was being written – it was not very pleasant, for instance, to have the *South Wales Argus* campaigning to replace me with David Bishop only a few months after I had been voted best European player at the 1987 World Cup – but I did not allow it to get personal with Robin Davey, their rugby writer, and accepted that he was doing the job asked of him by the paper.

The worst thing about being criticised in the papers is knowing that your family will see it, and that it will hurt them. On one occasion, during the 1991 World Cup, a newspaper report did cause me a few problems. The *Sunday People* ran a feature on a couple of girls who had been following Wales for years. They were always around, at games and at hotels before and after games, asking for autographs and to be photographed with us. Everybody knew them and we'd all been photographed with them – I was probably photographed a dozen times over seven or eight years. I don't think there was anything malicious about the story, but the timing was a bit unfortunate as they ran it on the day of the Western Samoa match, complete with about a dozen photographs of these women with the players. I was in three of them. We didn't see the paper before the game, so we can't blame it for our performance or the result. But it did make the evening afterwards more difficult than it should have been. I was confronted by Meg brandishing the paper and wanting to know what was going on. It was bad enough having lost to Western Samoa, but then to have to persuade my wife that my dealings with these women were totally above board was something I could really have done without.

There is a small minority in the tabloid press which is keen to stir things up and create scandal where it does not really exist, but luckily I have had no problems of this sort. I know that John Kennedy of the *Western Mail* was told to dig dirt during the 1995 World Cup, but he refused to do it. My own dealings with the *Sun*, as a columnist, have been very happy. Tony Roche and David Facey, the journalists I deal with, have never twisted anything I have said or tried to build it up into something it wasn't.

Letters to the press can also be very upsetting, and I do think papers have a duty to be careful about what they publish. You'll quite often get a dispute going in the letters pages. Somebody will write in attacking a player, there'll be a reply defending him, and then the original writer will hit back defending what he said. It is not very enjoyable to be the person they are writing about. The Swansea *Evening Post* once ran a letter from somebody called Kevin Jenkins writing from a Baglan address. It wasn't just critical of the way I was playing, it was an all-out attack on my abilities, personality and fitness to play for Wales. There was a reply, and then this Jenkins character hit back. I did not like it, and my parents were particularly upset. My mother even picked up the phone and complained to the editor. My father tried to obtain a telephone number for this Kevin Jenkins, and also checked the electoral register. He found there was nobody of that name living at the address given in the letters.

Everyone is entitled to his or her opinion, and it is something you have to live with as a player, but I was annoyed that the paper published personal attacks from someone who had given a false name and/or address. Papers have the right to publish letters expressing strong opinions about rugby, but I do think they should make sure the person who is apparently making those statements really exists –

and they should also learn to distinguish between constructive criticism, which must always be accepted, and personal attacks.

The papers also need to encourage the same attitude in their journalists. The people reporting the game, and in particular those who write columns, should know the game. That does not necessarily mean that they should have played at senior level – there are people who have developed a knowledge and understanding of the game over time without playing at any serious level – but it is an advantage. I have already mentioned Gerald and Clem as people who have put a deep knowledge of the game to the best possible use, and I also like Brynmor Williams' column in the *Evening Post*. He can be critical of players, but never maliciously, always constructively, putting any criticisms in the context of an intelligent analysis of what players are trying to achieve and the pressures and problems they face. Of course it does no harm that he is also a former scrum-half whose views on the game are often similar to my own!

This is the way things should be done. Of course it is reasonable to say that a player has had a bad game, but it is not acceptable to turn that into a personal attack. Having a bad game does not mean that you are a bad human being, or that you have let down your country. A problem that we have in Wales is that we do have enormous mood swings, and this is reflected in the letter pages and in the reporting. A player can be a national hero one week and a disgrace the next. Neil Jenkins has taken some appalling abuse during his career, and then suddenly he is regarded as one of the greatest living Welshmen with papers campaigning to get him a medal. Even somebody as strong-minded as Neil must have found this tough. People may say they don't take any notice of the papers, but I don't believe them. It is almost impossible not to take notice. Even if you do not, your family will.

At the same time, we cannot expect journalists to be cheerleaders for the national team or the club they are covering. If there are problems, they should be reporting them. Covering them up is the worst thing that can happen. I thought that Swansea Rugby Club were very unfair to Mark Orders, the rugby writer from the *Evening Post*, after the 2000/01 Heineken Cup quarter-final. The paper is an important supporter of Swansea and the other clubs it covers. Mark is always happy to support the club – if there is an event or function it wants publicised he will help – and I always found him an honest and balanced reporter. That also means saying when the team has played badly, as they did in that quarter-final against Leicester. As they showed in winning the competition, Leicester are an exceptional side and they were on their best form against Swansea, but the All Whites did play badly. No supporter would tell you any different, and Mark's comments reflected this. So I was disappointed that Dick Moriarty had a go at him.

There was a further incident when the *Evening Post* reported that there had been a public bust-up between John Plumtree, the club coach, and James Griffiths, who plays lock forward. John Plumtree was out for a drink with friends from New Zealand and they ran into James Griffiths, who is a talented player but has had problems with discipline. There were a few verbal exchanges and some pushing and shoving. This was seen by members of the public, and news of anything like this travels fast in Swansea. It was soon being written about on the club's website, and a couple of days later the *Evening Post* carried a report including a statement by the club secretary Byron Mugford that the incident had been dealt with, that it had looked worse than it really was and that James Griffiths and John Plumtree were now happily working together in training. The following weekend, after the match against Pontypridd, Plumtree refused to speak to journalists while Mark Orders was there.

You can't try to isolate your local paper like that. The *Evening Post* would have been failing in its duties as a local paper had it not reported the incident – just about everybody in Swansea knew about it, after all – and their report also gave the club the chance to say publicly that any problems had been sorted out. The irony is that Mark's report of the Pontypridd match, which explained that Plumtree had refused to speak to him, went on to say what an excellent job he had done as coach in getting the team back on track after its disappointments in the Heineken Cup. Mark was doing his job well. It was a pity Plumtree could not accept that.

Anyone who does go into journalism is likely to spend a fair amount of time watching the movements of the Welsh Rugby Union as it attempts to cope with the modern rugby world. It has done rather badly at this over the last few years, with the consequences this book has described. Yet the WRU committee has always included decent, talented people. The structures have been more at fault than most individuals. The current system, based on the districts, is too unwieldy. Instead of the current oversized committee, we should be looking towards the creation of an executive of around six people. As soon as the body gets up to eight or ten members it becomes unwieldy again.

We need to retain representation for the clubs – perhaps one member each drawn from the senior and junior clubs. We also need to retain an elected element, so executive members are answerable to the game in Wales. Whatever precise means is selected for choosing them, they need to be people of independent standing and talent, capable of running a serious sport in the twenty-first century. Some would certainly have business expertise. There are people like Chris Evans, who was instrumental in bringing Jonathan Davies back to Wales to play for Cardiff. He is an enormously successful businessman, and obviously a big rugby fan. It would be good to get people like him putting their skills and experience into helping to run the game. But business skills are not the only skills we need; knowledge of the game at every level, of the media and of rugby's international politics will also be important. As in the other areas of off-field activity discussed in this chapter, getting these things right would increase Wales's chances of getting things right on the field.

# **12** There's More to Life than Rugby

'Had I gone from school straight into being a professional player, as young players with the record I had in 1984 do nowadays, I would have missed out on experiences outside the world of rugby which are serving me very well nowadays as I try to develop a career away from the game. There is a lesson here for today's young players. Just because you have a professional contract, it does not mean that you should do nothing but play and train for rugby. There is a limit to how much time you can devote to training, and you certainly will not be able to play rugby all your life.'

I WOULD HAVE JUMPED AT THE CHANCE of being a professional rugby player when I was eighteen. I could have imagined nothing better. It was not as if very much else interested or motivated me at that age – as the rather sad saga of my A levels shows. And while I was not interested when an offer was made to play rugby league – there was never any chance I would take it, so the issue was not pursued – I was happy to take the chance of playing professionally towards the end of my career, at the age of thirty.

But I am not somebody who curses being born a dozen years too early, or looks with envy at current young players. Had I gone from school straight into being a professional player, as young players with the record I had in 1984 do nowadays, I would have missed out on experiences outside the world of rugby which are serving me very well nowadays as I try to develop a career away from the game. There is a lesson here for today's young players. Just because you have a professional contract, it does not mean that you should do nothing but play and train for rugby. There is a limit to how much time you can devote to training, and you certainly will not be able to play rugby all your life. I worked outside rugby because I had to. The modern player does not have to, but he would certainly benefit from even a couple of hours' work a week outside the game, developing experience and shifting the focus for a while.

Rugby has played an important role in my working career. Every opportunity I was given came as a result of rugby contacts. The employers I worked for were prepared to give me the flexibility I needed to play top-class rugby. I was lucky with that. Other players had employers who were not so accommodating, and their careers suffered as a result. But if rugby helped get me through certain doors, I still had to justify my presence. None of the jobs I did was a made-up post which allowed me to spend all day on the phone to friends before I went off to training. I had to be able to justify what my employers were paying me, not to mention the flexibility they allowed me. None was a large enough company to be able to carry passengers. And all of them gave me experience, skills and contacts that I have found useful in developing a business career.

My first job was as a filing clerk with John Morse solicitors in Swansea. Mike James, the chairman of Swansea Rugby Club, organised it for me. John is a hell of a nice guy and the business was quite interesting as well – he was involved in property development as well as the law. I won my first cap while I was working there, so the *Evening Post* ran pictures of me celebrating with a mug of tea with the secretaries in the office. I was grateful for the work and the money – with that and the travel expenses paid by the All Whites I was able to buy my first car – and I learned something about administration, clerical work and dealing with people. The problem was that it was not likely to take me anywhere or earn me qualifications – I was not going to become a solicitor, or even a solicitor's clerk – so it was never going to be a long-term option.

My next opportunity came through my Swansea colleague Malcolm Dacey – if you think there is a pattern emerging, you are right – to work for the OCS Group. My job was to assist Clive Thomas, the football referee, who was chair of OCS Group Wales. (Nowadays, Clive runs Caxton Facilities Management, an offshoot of OCS which he bought out some years ago.) In practical terms this meant being Clive's driver, as he was disqualified at the time. He had a yellow Mercedes which I occasionally brought home after a day's work. Since he was in charge of industrial relations in the group, we spent a lot of time driving to industrial tribunals all around the country. It was interesting sitting in on the hearings, which were like a court of law, with Clive acting like a legal counsel defending his company, explaining why somebody had been sacked.

Clive is a very interesting man. He has strong opinions on just about every subject you can think of, not just football. We got on well, and still do on the occasions when we meet, although we did not always see eye to eye. Clive had a thing about cars being kept clean. On one occasion I was driving him home in my car and he suddenly said, 'Why are we going towards Newport?' I replied, 'We're not going towards Newport. We're going the right way, towards your home.' After a moment, Clive replied, in a rather sarcastic manner, 'Sorry, I couldn't see through all the dirt on the windscreen.'

I could live with that, but I did find the amount of driving I had to do rather wearing. To start with I had to drive into work in Cardiff, and then we would go off to wherever Clive was involved in a hearing, which could be anywhere in Britain. We went as far afield as Scotland. That did get rather tedious, and I was also concerned about being able to fit in all the travelling with my rugby commitments.

So I was happy to move on to join my first Swansea captain, David Richards, who had set up his own finance company, County Leasing and Finance. He was looking for a rep to go on the road dealing with the motor trade in South Wales. The package was no better than what I was on at OCS, but it was based in Swansea, which was much more convenient for home and St Helen's. The other directors – Arwel Morgan, Russell Davies and Gordon Harris – were all big rugby men as well, so there was always flexibility in my routine. I really enjoyed the work, travelling around car dealerships, and I stayed for five and a half years. Life was relatively easy, but I think I earned my crust.

This job ended, ironically enough, not long after the company was taken over by BJ Group – Mike James's company. The idea was that I'd move across and work with BJ Group, but it did not work out and I began to think it was time for a change.

This time, the opportunity was offered by Gerallt Davies of Sterling Asset Management. Gerallt had employed Jonathan Davies and also Jonathan's brother-in-law Phil Davies. They were talking about opening an office in Swansea. Phil, who is a very good friend, completely genuine although not perhaps the most reliable person in the world, approached me about going in with him and I was taken with his enthusiasm for the idea. I could see real potential in it. Phil already knew the financial services sector well and I'd get the chance to learn about it and at the same time have the challenge of helping set up an office.

I decided to go for it. After a couple of weeks, a lot of which had been spent on training courses, Phil rang up and said he was leaving as he had found another job. I was a bit concerned about this, and I was right to be as I did not have the experience to carry the office by myself. Gerallt was very understanding and gave me all the support he could, but it was never easy.

After a few months, as luck would have it, another opportunity came along. 'Spider' Davies, who had been such a help to me when I first joined the All Whites, was by now chief executive of the Swansea Building Society and they decided they needed a business development executive to promote their mortgage and investment products. All of this was very valuable in terms of building up my own business knowledge and contacts, meeting people who were extremely successful and influential.

I gave that up to go to South Africa in 1994, but in between my two summers out there I started working for the insurance brokers C.E. Heath of Wales. The chairman of the company was Ian Price, secretary of the Crawshays Welsh, president of Abertillery and a former Cardiff second row, while the business development director, with whom I worked a lot, was Brynmor Williams.

Working with them further developed my contacts and experience. I had always envied and admired people like Dai Richards and Clive Thomas, who ran their own companies, and wanted to emulate them after I had packed up my boots. That opportunity came, with good timing, close to the end of my rugby career with the setting up of Sports Design Partnership. The concept was to design, supply and fit out sporting, leisure and fitness facilities, as a sort of one-stop shop. The other partners are Brian Taylor of Taylor Tiles of Swansea – where I have my office – Arnott Hughes, a partner in Lawray Architecture of Cardiff, and Wyn Jones, a former director of Barclays Bank. I became managing director at the end of last year when we decided someone had to devote themselves fully to take the project forward. I was the obvious person, given the commitments the other partners already had.

I am also involved in helping to develop the Welsh side of a company called Inside Rugby, a management and recruitment company set up by friends of mine, Alan Zondagh, Dick Best and Richard Stiles, but most of my time is devoted to SDP. I find my rugby profile helps in terms of getting opportunities, but it can be a drawback too. Sometimes people are reluctant to say no to you, and this can mean that your time and theirs is wasted when an order is not really likely. Overall, though, I have no doubt it has more pluses than minuses. My hope is that SDP will develop in time into a major company. We have no doubt there is a niche in the market for the services we are providing, and the experience so far has been very favourable. Some work has already been completed, and there is plenty more in the order book.

At the same time, I have been developing my work in sports journalism and broadcasting. I have had a column for the *Sun* since the 1999 World Cup. One concern about working for a tabloid was that they might want me to be critical for the sake of it or to deal with subjects that are not really related to the game, so I am pleased they have not gone down that route. I also work at weekends for Radio Five Live.

I really enjoy working for a major broadcaster and the fact that my work goes beyond the traditional role for ex-players – answering questions and summarising on the game. I have a proper reporting job, with responsibility for ensuring all the links are in place and that the studio is kept in touch with scores and other developments in the game. During a game, it could be that they'll tell me they are coming to me in a couple of minutes. It is then up to me to sum up what has happened in, say, twenty seconds, giving the facts rather than my views on the game, although final match reports do contain a few more views. Reports can be critical if I think it necessary, but it has to be honest, constructive and, I hope, helpful. I would like to do more of it. I hear of football reporters who work two or three times a week and I wish I could get that much practice, as I've no doubt you get better with more practice.

It was nerve-racking to start with – my notes blowing away one windy day in Bridgend did not help – but the trick is to try to relax and be yourself. There are still times when it feels a little strange to be on the other side of the fence – 'one of them', as players say – especially when I interview players who were team-mates recently (Andy Moore finished one interview by saying 'Thank you, Roberta'). But the radio work stopped me missing being a player, for a few months at least. It kept me occupied on Saturdays, and at the start I was so nervous about it that I did not have time to think about what I would be doing were I still a player.

As I became more relaxed about the radio work, I did start to miss playing a little, although not sufficiently to take up a couple of offers to come out of retirement. I played a match for Micky Steele-Bodger's XV against Cambridge University the week before the 2000 Varsity match and could not believe how good I felt, how easily things I had not practised for weeks were happening. Paul Turner and Mal Malik spent about three weeks trying to persuade me to come and play for them at Rugby for the rest of the season. My other offer, from Toulouse, came completely out of the blue. I was flattered that they believed I could come out of retirement and play such an incredibly physically demanding level of rugby as is found in the French championship, and I did think seriously about it – they were offering an extremely attractive package and the challenge was an exciting one – but I knew that I was never going to take it. I retired because I wanted to develop my work on the radio and my business career, and going back to playing would have meant neglecting them. But it was good to be asked.

Saying yes would also have been tough on my family. I am already busier than I have ever been, away for weekends for international matches and on Saturday when I cover club games, while the working week is more than full with Sports Design Partnership, Inside Rugby and the Dragons Rugby Trust. To have started travelling to France would have taken me away from Meg, Emily and Tiaan for even longer periods, and while all the work I am doing now is aimed at securing the best possible future for them, I do worry about spending enough time with them.

At least Meg knew what she was letting herself in for when she married a rugby player. Her mother, Margaret, is a very laid-back, easy-going person who has needed those qualities to accept the commitment Clive has given to rugby over the years. He has done just about every job in the game, as well as running his sports shop and working for different companies. Meg's memories of her childhood are far more of her mother. She used to call her father 'Uncle Clive' because he was not there very much! Knowing that rugby was the reason why he was away most weekends probably helped her adjust to my way of life.

The first times I saw Meg were at rugby matches – her cousin Ian Jeffries played alongside me at Swansea while her brother Dewi played for the local district side. But we first really met in a nightclub, Mamma Mia's in Pontardawe. It is still there, though it's called the Paradise Club now. It was Meg's birthday, 18 December, in 1984. I said I'd get in touch and she offered to give me her number. I said, 'Don't worry,

I'll find out,' thinking that as Clive Rowlands was such a well-known figure it should be easy to get it. I didn't realise it was ex-directory. In the end I got in my car and drove to Upper Cwmtwrch in the hope of spotting her in the street (I didn't know where their house was). I had nearly given up and was on my way home when, as luck would have it, she got out of a friend's car.

That was not the only time I had problems with that particular phone number. The following summer I was in Hong Kong with the Crawshays Welsh, an invitation team which claims to have the worst initiation ceremony in rugby (I can't say whether it lives up to this claim because you have to swear not to reveal what it is, but I will say that I was absolutely terrified beforehand). I had been trying to ring Meg ever since we'd got there, with no luck. After a while I realised what the problem was: for some reason I had been dialling the Swansea code, not the one for Upper Cwmtwrch. This dawned on me after a few drinks, which is how I came to be on the phone in a grocer's shop in Hong Kong, asking if they could give me the code for Upper Cwmtwrch. You may be surprised to learn that I was unsuccessful, and was hauled away by Kevin Hopkins, who assured me that there was no way in the world I was going to find out the Upper Cwmtwrch code in that shop. Always a source of sound advice, Kevin.

Meg and I were married in 1987, soon after the World Cup, but having already gone through the experience of a rugby-oriented lifestyle with her father didn't necessarily help her when it came to living with me. Having members of your family constantly subjected to public criticism wears you down after a while. It did not help that a lot of the time people who wanted to have a go at me would attack Clive as well, saying I was only in the team because he was my father-in-law.

Neither did things get any easier for my parents. My mother went to all of my internationals and until not so long ago would go to any game Ant, Rhod or I played in. But over the last few seasons she has gone much less, although my father still goes to watch Rhod play for Swansea. He and my mother will go down together into town, but while he goes to St Helen's she'll go shopping or take Emily and Tiaan for a walk. There is a limit to how much abuse you can hear your children taking, and she has reached it. Afterwards, she is delighted to hear if Rhod has had a good game, but if it did not go well and the crowd were on his back, she does not want to know.

But all these trials and tribulations paled into insignificance when, in the summer of 1999, Meg and I and Rhodri and his girlfriend (now wife) Helen, on our way back in a taxi from Paul Arnold's wedding do in Morriston, were involved in a nasty crash with a police car. It was just after midnight and we were coming back past the Inco golf course (like everyone else in the area, I still think of it as the Mond course) in Clydach, only a few hundred yards from home. I was sitting in the front seat and had turned round to talk to Meg, who was sitting behind the driver, because I could not find the keys and thought she might have them in her bag. Suddenly, all hell broke loose. There was an almighty crash, the taxi driver shouted something, and by the time I'd started to turn round to see what was happening the windscreen had shattered. That is all I remember until I came round several minutes later.

In the meantime, Meg had hauled herself out of the car and run round to the front. She could see me slumped in my seat, out cold, and could not get my door open. She thought I was dead. She ran to the smashed-up police car and found the passenger motionless and the driver in a very bad way. By chance, a friend from Trebanos, Trudi Frost, had been travelling just behind us and stopped to help. Trudi has since said that she thought I was dead as well, and her main throught was to get Meg away from the car.

When I came round, I have to say I have never felt weaker or more helpless. I was unable to lift my arm or move my head. The seat belt had knocked everything out of me and it was a struggle to breathe. I could hear the driver, who was wedged up against his seat by the steering wheel, moaning and groaning. Rhodri, whose arm was broken in four places, was crying from the pain and at the same time shouting out to see how I was. There was a light on in the car, but I was finding it difficult to focus.

I'd improved a little by the time the police and ambulance arrived. They had to check I was OK before they moved me and I did my best to reassure them as I got more air back into my body. Then they pulled me out and led me across to the ambulance. I didn't look back. I didn't really want to know how bad it looked and I had a pain in my chest from a fractured sternum.

I could see Rhodri sitting on the side of the road, holding his arm. Helen had been in a panic about the petrol on the road from the cars and had been shouting to get us all out. It is incredible how the adrenalin gets to you on an occasion like this. Helen had a compound fracture of the foot which needed a lot of treatment and has left her with scars and a slight limp, but she had still been able to haul herself out of the car and shout to the rest of us to get away as well. Meg's ankles were injured – her feet had been driven up under the driver's seat in the crash – but she too had still been able to get out and run over first to my door and then to the other car.

We got into the ambulance. Rhodri was saying, 'My arm's broken' – he had lost his chance to play in the World Cup, and possibly of ever playing for Wales – while Helen was asking, 'What happened?' The policeman who had been driving the other car, and who had serious internal injuries, was also in the ambulance with us. At the hospital we learned that his passenger had died. Rhodri and Helen were taken away for emergency X-rays and Meg was put in a wheelchair. Then the shock started to come through. She started to shake and could not stop.

Meg was kept in for a couple of hours. I left the following morning, but Rhodri and Helen had to stay in for a couple of days. The mental trauma was worse than the physical injuries. I was in a complete daze for three or four days. Clive and Margaret came to stay for a couple of days to help my parents look after us. Meg and I did not want to talk about what happened; we spent most of the time just lying down, not saying anything.

It was a frightening experience. It put me off driving for a while – I could not drive at all for three weeks – and ended my career at Cardiff. It knocked all the enthusiasm for the game out of me for quite a time and made the thought of driving to Cardiff every day intolerable. The experience is still with Meg. She has nightmares about the accident and has become an extremely nervous passenger. I pass the site of the accident almost every day. The worst part of it, though, is thinking about the policeman who was killed, a fate that could easily have been ours. His name was Ian Godfrey, and he had two children about the same age as Emily. They went to bed one night and when they woke up they had no father. Meg has kept in touch with his widow, Samantha, and tried to give any support she can. It still frightens me to think how easily Emily might have been left without parents at the age of seven.

Meg and I knew even when we were courting that we would not be able to have children in the normal way, although we did go for tests after we were married to see if there might be scope for using alternative methods. It never seemed likely, and we put ourselves down as adoptive parents as soon as we were married. Adoption is a long process. We were told that it might take up to ten years, so perhaps we were lucky that we only had to wait half that time for Emily. The process is also very intrusive. They do every possible check on you and question you on every aspect of your lives, about your relationship, your sex life, anything that could possibly affect your ability to be parents. It did help a little that I was used to being questioned by journalists – admittedly on rather different subjects – and held up to scrutiny. And through it all you of course understand why they have to take every possible precaution against children falling into the wrong hands.

Emily arrived in January 1993. She was eight months old and had been with foster parents. I can't imagine that birth parents feel any different emotionally to the way we did that day. People talk about growing to love someone, but if you have been waiting as long for a child and wanted one as much as we did, the effect is immediate. It was the same for my parents, who had been a little unsure and nervous about our adopting. They loved Emily the moment they saw her; the bond my mother had with her from day one was incredible. Clive and Margaret have always been one hundred per cent supportive too, so Emily has been very lucky in her grand-parents.

She is as much part of a wide, very close family as any of her cousins, a fact which was demonstrated when she was chosen to be the mascot for the All Whites in an evening match against Neath. It was a big match, live on television in Wales, and Rhodri was at scrum-half for Neath. We still went out to practise together that afternoon, throwing the ball back and forth and getting loosened up, as we always did even when we were opponents. When we ran out I carried Emily on and put her down in the middle of the field. She probably felt a bit lost, and looked around for a while. The first person she saw was Uncle Rhodri, and she ran across to him. Rhod picked her up and ran with her back to the touchline, very much the proud uncle, showing everyone how close a family we are.

You might expect the adoption process to be easier the second time round, but if anything it is tougher. On the first occasion there is no parenting track record to go by when making the decision about suitability; now they had plenty of material. Emily was interviewed, and so were her teachers and our friends. And it was worth every moment when our son Tiaan Rhodri, who is now a toddler, arrived.

You have your ups and downs with children. Tiaan has not always been the world's greatest sleeper, and Emily is a slow starter in the morning. She likes to disappear into the toilet for half an hour when Meg is desperately trying to get her ready to be collected for school by my cousin Angharad. I must admit there are times when I'm happy to be out early to escape all the trauma, but of course none of that matters against the happiness of having two beautiful children.

They are growing up in a world where rugby matters. Emily has been a mascot and seen her father and uncle playing senior rugby; my father is already practising with Tiaan. Perhaps every proud father thinks similarly, but Tiaan does seem to kick and throw well for a child his age. It certainly would be something to have a Wales scrum-half whose father, grandfather and three uncles (Dewi, who won youth caps, Ant and Rhod) had all worn the red number nine shirt at some level before him!

It would delight me if they did grow up to love and perhaps play the game. Now that women's rugby is growing in popularity, Emily will also get the chance to play if she wants. But that is entirely up to them. Having a family is a constant reminder to me that there are more important things in life than rugby, just as there are events which matter more to Wales than any international match. That said, I hope that as they grow up they will have the chance I and many Welsh youngsters before me had of seeing our national team matching the best in the world on the rugby pitch, and doing it by playing the skilled, expansive game that has caught the Welsh imagination and won the respect of the rest of the world for most of the past century. That tradition and style of rugby inspired me as it inspired Jonathan Davies, Gareth Edwards, Cliff Morgan and the succession of players who have created and sustained it. One reason for writing this book is the hope that it can be rescued and once again put on display, to inspire my children and the generations to come.

# Index